The Elder Lat

Ramón Valle
and
Lydia Mendoza

With the Assistance of
Community Interviewers:

Sra. María Dutra
Sra. Herminia Enrique
Sra. Martha García
Sr. Antonio Guerrero
Sra. Enriqueta Hay
Sra. Hilda Nazario-Lindsey
Sra. Lilia López
Sra. Marcelina Nuñez
Sra. Casilda Pagan
Sra. Luz Valenzuela

Technical Consultants:

Charles Martinez
Maria Zuñiga de Martinez

Center on Aging, San Diego State University

The Elder Latino

A CROSS-CULTURAL STUDY OF MINORITY ELDERS IN SAN DIEGO

Editor & Project Director:	Ramón Valle, PhD
Project Director:	James Ajemian, PhD (First Year)
Associate Editor:	Charles Martinez, MSW
Secretaries:	Mrs. Peggy King
	Mrs. Patricia Murphy
	Mrs. Alicia Nevarez-Krotky
	Ms. Cynthia Wright
Cover:	Mr. Calvin Woo, Humangraphics
Published By:	Center on Aging
	School of Social Work
	San Diego State University
Design Style & Phototypeset:	Betty R. Truitt
	Word Processing Center
	San Diego State University

Monographs and Technical Reports Series

The Elder American Indian:	Frank Dukepoo, PhD
The Elder Black:	E. Percil Stanford, PhD
The Elder Chinese:	Ms. Eva Cheng, MSSW
The Elder Guamanian:	Wesley H. Ishikawa, DSW
The Elder Japanese:	Ms. Karen C. Ishizuka, MSW
The Elder Latino:	Ramón Valle, PhD
	Ms. Lydia Mendoza, MS
The Elder Pilipino:	Ms. Roberta Peterson, MSSW
The Elder Samoan:	Wesley H. Ishikawa, DSW

Project Supported by Funds from U.S. Department of Health, Education and Welfare, Office of Human Development, Administration on Aging. Grant Number AoA-90-A-317, Mr. David Dowd, Project Officer AoA, OHD, DHEW.

Distributed by The Campanile Press, San Diego State University

Library of Congress Cataloging Data
Catalog Card No.: 77-83498
Valle, Ramón
The Elder Latino
San Diego, Calif.: Campanile Press
p. 114
7708   770708

ISBN 0-916304-32-9

Distributed for the Center on Aging by
The Campanile Press
San Diego State University
5300 Campanile Drive
San Diego, California
92182

/ R. Valle & L. Mendoza|

Acknowledgments

We are in debt to our interviewers, who assisted us well beyond their assigned responsibilities. We are equally in debt to our community consultants, Sr. Jorge Valle, Sra. Anna Ramírez, Sr. Felipe Munduate, Sra. Marina Sánchez, Sr. Ramón González, and Sra. Guadalupe Zuñiga who opened doors for us and who are constantly in service to Latinos, particularly the elderly. We are also very appreciative of the organization of Latino Seniors, Inc., of San Diego whose board and members assisted throughout the life of the project.

We wish to thank Dr. Fernando Torres-Gil, Dr. Lynne Riehman and Professora Maria Zuñiga de Martinez for their thoughtful reviews of the draft versions of this document, as well as Mr. Paul Espinosa who assisted substantially in editing this report. We equally appreciate the assistance of Mr. Daniel Martinez in reviewing the methodological formulation contained in this report.

There are also a number of other persons who have had varying degrees of impact to the project as a whole from the proposal stage to the end. Dr. Gideon Horowitz was instrumental in developing the proposal for which initial funds were received. Dr. James Ajemian assumed the directorship for the project during its first year. Mr. Charles Martinez provided extremely helpful technical support throughout the process of the research, especially at the point of finalizing the monographs. Dr. Roger Cunniff, Mrs. Sharon Swinscoe and Gerald Thiebolt of The Campanile Press were most helpful in extending their assistance throughout the process of publishing this editorial serial of reports. We wish also to recognize the School of Social Work of San Diego State University under whose general auspices the study was conducted. The researchers are equally appreciative of the continual support from the Administration on Aging by Mr. David Dowd, Project Officer.

We are grateful to all of the above for their involvement in this research effort.

Dedication

We are especially grateful to our respondents who spoke to us with persisting eloquence.

A Los Profesores

Profesores, con placer
y buscando algun pretesto
los quisiera conocer y
darle las gracias por esto

Tocante a mi información,
no creo que valga nada
esa es mi opinión
pero ya está sentada.

Y en retorno a sus favores
le manifiesto otra vez,
que tienen más un servidor
porque les acepté los diez.

Esto queda entre nosotros
y no me echen la viga
esto se los pagará Dios
y que El mismo los bendiga.

Printed with permission of
the author, Sr. Antonio Perez,
Latino component respondent.

Table of Contents

I. INTRODUCTION TO THE STUDY*

Cross-Cultural Study on Minority Elders
Research Objectives

This study of Latino older persons is part of a larger Cross-Cultural Study of Minority Elders of San Diego County. The study extended over a two-year period, 1974-1976, and was funded by the Administration on Aging (AoA), of the Office of Human Development (OHD), Department of Health, Education and Welfare (DHEW). In addition to Latinos, seven other populations of minority elders were part of the research. These included, American Indian, black, Chinese, Guamanian, Japanese, Pilipino, and Samoan elders. The study as a whole adopted a common methodology with a set of common objectives in mind. These could be stated in the following terms:

- To explore and describe the characteristic lifestyles and primary interactional networks of ethnic minority older people.
- To identify perceptions and attitudes of ethnic minority elders toward formal programmatic assistance and analyze the relationship between the characteristic lifestyles and the use and perception of formal assistance.
- To design and test a methodology adopted for appropriateness and effectiveness in obtaining information about ethnic populations, specifically the elders of these populations.

The Study Site

The study was conducted within the County of San Diego, which is designated as a Complete Standard Metropolitan Statistical Area (SMSA) by the Bureau of Census. The total SMSA encompasses approximately 4,296 square miles and an estimated 1.5 million persons. To the south, it borders Baja California and the Mexican city of Tijuana. Orange County forms the northern border to the SMSA, with the Los Angeles metropolitan complex then being immediately adjacent. San Diego to a large extent forms the nexus of a well-traveled commercial corridor which stretches some 200 miles from Los Angeles through to Ensenada in Baja California.

The Elderly in San Diego

At the initiation of the study, the researchers had varying estimates of the elderly population of the SMSA and opted to utilize the 1975 projections of San Diego County Area Agency on Aging which were based on the age 60-plus population. Of the total San Diego population, 1.5 million, approximately 198,300 or 13.2 percent were designated as 60-plus years (see Table 1).

Approximately 23,900 (11.9 percent) of the estimated 198,300 aged 60-plus elderly have been classified as ethnic-minority elders, (see Table 2). It must be noted, though, that the data regarding the ethnic elderly in San Diego were seen as "best estimates" only. Such census information was seen as essentially flawed on two counts: **namely, undercounts and mislabeling**. These issues as specifically related to the Latino elderly are discussed below.

Table 1

San Diego SMSA Age 60-Plus Population Estimates
$N = 1,500,000$

Population age	f	%
Under 60 years	1,302,000	86.8
Over 60 years	198,300	13.2

SOURCE: San Diego County Area Agency on Aging, formerly the Office of Senior Citizen Affairs, updated 1975 estimates.

Table 2

San Diego SMSA Age 60-Plus *
Population Estimates By Ethnic Groups

Group	f	Percent of Total Age 60-Plus Population $N = 198,300$	Percent of Minority 60-Plus Population By Ethnic Minority Group $n = 23,900$*
Anglo/White	174,400	87.9	
Latino	14,900	7.5	62.3
Black	4,500	2.2	18.8
Pilipino	1,300	0.6	5.4
Japanese	700	0.4	2.9
American Indian	500	0.3	2.0
Chinese	300	0.2	1.4
Samoan	300	0.2	1.4
Guamanian	200	0.1	0.8
Other ethnic minorities not clearly designated	1,200	0.6	5.0

*NOTE: The Area Agency on Aging estimates of specific ethnic minority populations have been further updated with best estimates available from organizations serving each population.

The Latino Study Population

An analysis of project funds and time available, as well as the methodology to be utilized, indicated that a study population of approximately 600 total subjects would be feasible. In fact, 628 ethnic minority persons were interviewed. Table 3 summarizes the cross-cultural study population by specific ethnic designation. The further heterogeneity of each specific minority group studied along with the principal findings are described in the series of monographs commissioned through the research project.

/ R. Valle & L. Mendoza|

Table 3

AoA Study Population

N = 628

Group	f	%
Latino	218	34.7
Black	101	16.1
Pilipino	74	11.8
American Indian	62	9.8
Japanese	60	9.6
Chinese	50	7.9
Samoan	40	6.4
Guamanian	23	3.7

Although the Latino elderly comprise approximately two-thirds (62.3 percent) of all the estimated minority elderly in San Diego, they formed only about one-third (34.7 percent) of the total study population. Here again, as is outlined in Part II, the research intent intervened. To have proceeded with population sampling solely on a numerically proportionate basis would have meant that the size of the Latino sample would have precluded obtaining representative content from the other ethnic minorities.

The Research Approach

A common methodology was utilized by all the groups within the Cross-Cultural Study on Minority Elderly. An inductive information building approach, as emphasized by Glaser and Strauss (1967) was developed. The overall intent was to build both a methodology and a data base for further gerontological research among ethnic minority groups. This led to the present reporting format which described in some detail the research decisions and practices at each step of the process.

Each minority component had a group of university-based researchers who acted as coordinators, and community-based interviewers in numbers adequate to the size of each the ethnic cohort included in the study. A research decision appropriate to the methodology had indicated that researchers of the same ethnicity would operate within their respective cohorts. This strategy permitted the tailoring of the research instruments and community contact patterns specifically to the linguistic and situational differentials to be encountered within each ethnic cohort. This approach also allowed the translation of the interview guides into the idiom appropriate to the ethnic group to be studied.

Fortunately, the concept of providing for a match between the ethnicity of the researcher and study population had been built into the original proposal and budget, although not in the fineline detail necessitated at the point of actual implementation. In its totality, the research group numbered ten university-based and twenty-eight community-based interviewers who had the support of one full-time technical assistant and three clerical staff.

Latino Component: Specific Objectives

As was permissible, the Latino component responded more specifically to issues emerging from this community. In reviewing the literature related to Latino research and Latino aging, two critical priorities emerged. The first was the need for the development of an appropriate methodology for dealing with Latino populations. The second was the need for the documentation of cultural processes and the cultural values of selected subgroups, especially the aged. Given the preceding considerations, the researchers then set the following specific objectives for the Latino component:

1. To design and test an alternative field research methodology.
2. To develop a baseline information profile which could be used for future comparative study with other Latino elderly populations.
3. To identify and explore indicators of ethnic identity with particular attention to ethnic self-designations.
4. To identify Latino elderly primary networks, particularly in terms of their supportive and non-supportive features.
5. To identify the expressed needs of the Latino study population with particular attention to the modes of coping with these needs.
6. To explore the Latino elders' attitudes toward helping and being helped.
7. To delineate the critical paths taken to and from the formal services.
8. To describe aspects of life satisfaction to be found among Latino elders as these might impact their overall outlooks and behaviors.

Supportive Literature and Latino Community Issues

The specific direction of the Latino component within the larger cross-cultural study was heavily influenced both by a review of the literature and by community concerns. Over the past decade, Latino gerontologists and researchers have raised three central issues in the literature: (1) the need for culturally appropriate research methodologies; (2) the need for research to identify cultural attitudes and behaviors; and (3) the need to address the problems attendant to the identification and enumeration of Latino populations. A fourth concern which became apparent to the researchers at the onset of the study was the issue of continued apprehension about research and the actions of researchers by minority communities.

Appropriate research methodology.

Torres-Gil (1972, 1974), Montiel (1975) and Maldonado (1975), all stress the development of other than conventional research methods for use with Latino elders. In this regard, Sotomayor (1973:159) calls on the researcher to obtain "cultural sanction" for any research done among Latino elderly. Torres-Gil (1974:112) and Cuellar (1974:8) expand Sotomayor's concept to a more specific recommendation. They stress the inclusion of Latino community participation at all the stages of the research: design, implementation, data analysis and dissemination. Collectively, the writers recommend against the use of Hispanic community members *solely* as subjects for research. As added features, Sotomayor (1975) and Solis (1975) point to the fact that the researchers must be significantly aware of local and regional languages as well as custom differentials.

In calling for the development of research innovations, these same Latino gerontologists indicate the need to guard against myth building. Maldonado (1975:213) is quite explicit. He asks that investigators not be blinded by old (social science) stereotypes. At the same time, he warns not to create new ones. He observes that Latino elders may not only be misunderstood by the general society but by their own culture as well. Such cautionary reminders are in keeping with other Hispanic researchers (Rios, 1968; Romano, 1968; Rocco, 1970; and Vaca, 1970) who have been quick to critique stereotypic studies conducted by Latinos and non-Latinos alike, while nonetheless recommending the development of culturally compatible research approaches in the social sciences. The San Diego research effort is an attempt to carry out this multiple charge.

The Latino concern with methodology found an echo among other ethnic minority researchers (Hamilton, 1973; Murase, 1972; and Takagi, 1972) as well as among ethnic majority investigators (Clark and Anderson, 1967; Blauner, 1973; and Moore, 1971, 1973). This concern was also grounded in the previous data-gathering experiences of the San Diego study project staff within their respective ethnic communities. These experiences had brought home the importance of attention to methodological detail and inclusion of community participation in the research effort.

Cultural attitudes and behaviors.

With regard to cultural content, the Latino literature indicates the need to document "traditional values" (Torres-Gil, 1972:79) and "cultural strengths" rather than "cultural barriers" (Sotomayor, 1971, 1973, 1975; Solis, 1975). The same literature stresses the need to first explore the normal relational and coping patterns of Latino elders (Cuellar, 1974; Sotomayor, 1971, 1975) before proceeding to study their interactions with human service delivery systems. In the collective opinion of these authors, indigenous processes and strengths have not yet been extensively identified and reported.

The policy literature related to Latino elderly supports this concern. Repeatedly, this material stresses the need for cultural information for decision making on the development and delivery of bilingual/bicultural services (Dieppa, 1969). Gómez, Martin and Gibson (1973), Hernández (1973), *The U.S. Senate Special Committee Hearings on Aging* (Parts I-V, 1968), *The Spanish Speaking Elderly Special Concerns Report* (White House Conference, 1971), and *First National Conference on Spanish Speaking Elderly Proceedings (1975)* are also replete with voices speaking to this issue. Speaking to this overall concern with bilingual/bicultural services, Reynoso and Coppleman (1972) make a distinction between the availability and accessibility of services. Services may be available but unaccessible because potential consumers lack knowledge of their presence and/or how to use them.

Agreeing with this latter distinction, the San Diego researchers decided it would be important to describe in depth the paths taken by the study respondents to services rather than simply to list frequencies of use. It was also felt that if the Latino respondents' cultural attitudes toward helping or being helped were identified, more effective programs could be designed which would make services not only *available* but also *accessible*.

Enumeration problems.

At the start of the inquiry, an extensive review of census information about Latinos in general and Latino seniors in particular revealed major enumeration problems affecting research with such populations. These difficulties were of three kinds: (1) difficulties arising from extensive undercounting of Latino populations; (2) difficulties stemming from mislabeling of Latino populations; and (3) the use of noncomparable sampling formats in the 1970 Dicennial Census.

Undercounts. By its own admission, the Bureau of the Census has acknowledged an undercount by as much as a 38 percent of Latinos of Mexican origin and by 6.6 percent of Spanish origin Latinos in the 1970 Census (*Bureau of Census Series*, P.20, No. 259, p. 3). A related element affecting undercounts is the factor of *undocumented workers*. As of 1976, a private research firm on contract to the Immigration and Naturalization Service (INS) estimated 8 million undocumented workers in the United States with 5.2 million (65 percent) noted as Mexican Nationals (*Los Angeles Times,* 1977:3). The INS' own estimate indicates a more conservative figure of 6 million undocumented workers but admits to a yearly influx of 500,000 to 1 million such persons (ibid.). A recent San Diego study placed an estimated 91,138 *undocumented workers* in the San Diego County study area (Villapando et al., 1977:x). How many such persons are elderly is not indicated but researchers found no evidence that the overall census totals of Latino aged in the study area had taken this factor into account.

Mislabeling. Hernández, Estrada and Alverez (1973) point out that formidable problems arise in the labeling practices of the Bureau of Census regarding Latino propulations. In some instances, Latinos are dumped into the category of *white*—this is particularly true of the 100 percent sampling formats (p. 672). This factor was corroborated by the United States Civil Rights Commission Study, which indicates that respondents were asked to report their color or race in terms of "White, Negro or Black, Indian American, Japanese, Chinese, Pilipino, Hawaiian, Korean or other" (*Counting the Forgotten*, 1974). Latinos were not given the opportunity to identify their ethnicity within this format.

Yet within other sampling formats, a host of varying identifications were possible. As Hernández and his associates report, such labels as Spanish surname, foreign-born, or foreign parentage were used as criteria for deciding whether a person was deemed of Latino heritage.

The question of origins and direct self-identification is further compounded in census data subsequent to 1970. For example, the 1970 Dicennial Census had one category denoting origin with regard to persons of Mexican heritage. The March 1972 data had two, *Mexicano* and *Chicano*. The March 1973 and March 1975 data provide for four labels, *Mexican American, Chicano, Mexican,* and *Mexicano (Bureau of Census Report,* P.20, No. 259, 1976). The labeling problems are further aggravated when one expands the research scope to include Latino populations other than those of Mexican heritage.

Sampling. In essence, the 1970 census utilized four distinct sampling formats in arriving at its estimates of Latino populations:

Format A   *100 percent sampling format*. This format was utilized as an attempt to collect basic population and housing information about every person and housing unit. With regard to discerning racial or ethnic identification, of the 20 items within the questionnaire, one question *(color or race)* was related to this area.

Format B   *20 percent sampling format*. In the process of obtaining the above basic information from every person and housing unit, a randomly selected 20 percent of the total 100 percent surveyed were asked 15 additional questions. Of these additional 15 questions, one item *(state or country of birth)* was relevant to discerning ethnic or racial identification.

Format C   *15 percent sampling format*. For some of the tabulations of the 1970 census of population, a subsample of three-quarters of the original 20 percent sample schedules was selected. This subsample was selected by a computer using a stratified, systematic sample design. Questionnaires utilized in this sample included 13 additional items to supplement the number of items used for the 20 percent sample. of these 13 items, two *(country of birth or parents' mother tongue)* were related to determining ethnic racial designation.

Format D   *5 percent sampling format*. For some tabulations of the 1970 census of population, a subsample of one-quarter of the original 20 percent sample schedules was selected. As in the 15 percent sampling format, this subsample was selected by a computer using a stratified, systematic sample design. In this sample, 17 questionnaire items were added to the total number of questions utilized in the 15 percent sample. Three of these items *(Spanish origin or descent; citizenship; and year of immigration)* were related to identifying ethnic or racial designation.

(Format analysis have been drawn from three combined resources, *Indicators of the Status of the Elderly in the United States*, DHEW Publication No. (OHD) 214-200 80, 1974; Hernández, Estrada and Alvarez, 1973; and *Counting the Forgotten*, 1974.)

As can be seen, despite the apparent chain of logic running between sampling formats, each asks distinctly different questions regarding ethnicity. The questions are different enough in kind so as to yield quite different information, about the same population for subsequent users of the census data. Attempts to separate out a coherent picture of Latino elderly within this disarray are quite problemmatical.

Shifting population estimates.

One immediate consequence of census difficulties is the reality of shifting population estimates. Table 4 illustrates the Bureau of Census' own changing enumerations of Latino populations, which indicate a gradual increase from 9 million in 1970 to 10.5 million in 1973 and 11.2 million in 1975.

Table   4

Differential Enumeration of Number of Persons
of Latino Origin from 1970, March 1973 and March 1975

Type of Spanish origin	1970 Census	1973 number	% change since 1970	1975 number	% change since 1970
Total Spanish origin	9,072,602	10,577,000	+16.6	11,202,000	+23.5
Mexican	4,532,435	6,293,000	+38.8	6,690,000	+47.6
Puerto Rican	1,429,395	1,548,000	+ 8.3	1,671,000	+16.9
Cuban	544,600	733,000	+34.6	743,000	+36.4
Central or South American	1,508,866	597,000	−60.4	671,000	−55.5
Other Spanish	1,057,305	1,406,000	+33.0	1,428,000	+35

NOTE: The table is a composite analysis from data presented in the following sources: U.S. Bureau of the Census, *Current Population Reports, Population Characteristics, Persons of Spanish Origin in the United States: March, 1973*, (Advance Report), Series P.20, No. 259, January 1974, (Reprint), p.3). U.S. Bureau of the Census, *Current Population Reports, Persons of Spanish Origin in the United States: March 1975*, Series P.20, No. 290, February 1976, p.3). Labels used in the sources have been retained.

A similar type of discrepancy was also readily verified within the San Diego SMSA data. The 1970 census data on Latino elderly in San Diego lists 8,065 persons age 60 or more years. The 1975 data places the Latino age 60-plus population at 14,890. This provides for an 84.6 percent discrepancy in gross population figures alone. In such instances though, local study area information appears more reliable based on first-hand interaction with the study groups. Given these choices the present inquiry proceeded with the San Diego County Area Agency on Aging population estimates of Latinos.

The Issue of Community Apprehension

Community apprehension with the research effort emerged as another very real concern, both for the total project and specifically with regard to the Latino component. Evidence of community apprehension with the research project emerged while it was still at the proposal stage. The minutes of meetings held in 1975 between the project initiators and representatives of San Diego minority constituencies highlight this factor along with suggestions for overcoming this apprehension. An implicit recommendation drawn from these records was the suggestion for the formation of a community advisory process once the project was funded.

Evidence of Latino community apprehension surfaced in two actual incidents during the course of the study. The first took place during the May 1975 data gathering period, and almost resulted in shutting down the research in the Logan Heights area of San Diego, located in Major Statistical Area (MSA) "O." The crisis was precipitated by the fact that the Latino component interviewers had been preceded by individuals who had been fraudulently signing up Latino seniors for a nonexistent insurance program. The interviewers were mistaken for this group, and the research effort had to be halted for some days until the matter could be cleared up. This involved much behind-the-scene meetings and telephoning between the project coordinators and field staff with key

/ R. Valle & L. Mendoza |

organizations in the affected area, who in turn communicated a corrected message to potential interviewees.

The second incident occurred after the completion of the project. In this case, the project coordinators could not quite understand the reluctance of the relative of one project staff members to travel to Los Angeles with the research group. Despite the close relationship between the project coordinators and the affected individual, several lengthy conversations over a three-week period were actually needed before the reason became apparent. Approximately 45 miles north of downtown San Diego, at San Onofre, the United States Immigration and Naturalization Service (INS) maintains a checkpoint. All passenger vehicles are slowed and scrutinized. Suspected vehicles are stopped. On any given day one may pass several vehicles with persons of Mexican appearance detained along the side of the checkpoint. Despite the fact that the affected individual had a sixty-year record of legal residence in the United States, fear of the checkpoint was seen as a real barrier to travel away from the San Diego area.

While anecdotal in nature, these incidents are utilized here to illustrate the problems faced by researchers entering the field among Latino populations. From the onset, the research group found that they could not ignore the potential element of fear or apprehension by community residents in the design of the study. The literature on Latinos does provide some verification of the presence of the distrust factor. Atencio (1971) points out a self-protectiveness among Latinos against outsiders and professionals—even professionals from one's own ethnic group—because of the past history of negative interfacing between Latinos and services, as well as information-gathering systems.

Community apprehension has also been voiced in other locales, as witnessed in the position taken by the Boston Black United Front in the early 1970's.

> The black community has been aware for some time that the research findings of social and biological scientists are increasingly being used to justify political and legal decision-making, the major consequences of which too often affect members of black communities in a negative manner. This fact makes it essential that all those responsible for research projects that may involve such uses pay careful attention to these issues in the planning, conduct, and reporting of their research, and that black communities exercise a vigilance where the conduct of research involving black people is concerned.
>
> A large majority of social science investigators who conduct research projects in black communities are insensitive to the many political issues that their research necessarily entails, while most of these investigators are also insensitive to cultural nuance which is a necessary part of any well-conceived and conducted research involving black people. This is a crucial situation for the black community, for if an investigator obtains results that, for one reason or another, are inaccurate, or if the results of his investigations are used by people in powerful positions to effect abhorrent policies, the investigator may only find his professional reputation tarnished. However, the people who are the recipients of the false conclusions or abhorrent policies, usually poor black people, find their lives—psychologically and physically—in extreme danger. (Boston Black United Front, 1970:17.)

With such issues well in mind but with confidence that feasible research alternatives were indeed at hand, the project staff proceeded to the design and implementation of the study.

II. Methodology

Theoretical Overview

The study proceeded on the strength of alternative methodological approaches which have been building in the social sciences for some time. These approaches represent a wide cross-section of related disciplines and a wide range of theorists, including members of the gerontological community. The special emphasis within the San Diego inquiry was to mesh several converging theoretical formulations into a single cohesive research strategy.

Contextual data collection.

Such theorists as Kurt Lewin (1936) and his "field theory" formulation were seen as opening the door to a core notion within the study, namely, that of "contextual analysis" of data. Lewin postulated a mode of analysis where discrete data would be interpreted in the context of the environments from which they were drawn. During this same period, Kardiner, a psychiatrist, and Linton, an anthropologist, (1945), experimented with research which analyzed discrete psychological events and attitudes in terms of their natural cross-cultural ambience. At later points, a number of theorists expanded the concept further; witness Judd and Marmor (1956), Kaplan (1971), Leighton (1961 and 1965), Murphy (1965) and von Bertalanaffy (1972).

Primary group information: natural systems research.

The contextual data collection approach placed the research into the path of tapping into what Spicer (1971) calls persistent identity systems which respond around a shared language, shared values and shared interactional patterns. From the gerontological perspective, Solomon (1974:9), terms this approach as research which focuses on "ethno systems". She speaks of such systems as small groups and collectivities of individuals whose ethnicity serves to define them and their relationship to the larger society. Both notions were seen as most appropriate to the groups selected for the San Diego inquiry.

From a more specific methodological standpoint, the research was geared to collect what Cooley (1909) terms primary group behaviors and what Garfinkel (1969) calls the "routine grounds of everyday activity." This meant proceeding in terms of what Mazda (1969) calls the "researcher's naturalistic stance," and in terms of what Schatzman and Strauss (1973) identify as the "natural ongoing environment."

Collectively these ideas either stemmed from or corresponded closely to the ethno-methodological research approach which is concerned with tying into and reporting accurately the way subjects typically organize everyday knowledge, Pfohl (1975:250). In this manner, Garfinkel (1967) and Cicourel (1970, 1972) with their ethno-methodological attention to linguistic/communicational processes were seen as especially significant to the Latino component of the study. Herbert Blumer's Symbolic Interaction formulation (1969) served also as an equally significant theoretical input. His focus on studying value processes in their actual situational context was seen as ideally meeting the concerns of Latino researchers in unlocking information about long standing enculturated and interactional patterns from the Hispanic respondents.

It should be noted that "natural networks" primary support systems have also received research attention within gerontological circles. Blau (1956), Shanas (1973) and Bild and Havighurst (1976) represent only several researchers focusing on these phenomena among the elderly.

Combined data collection methods.

These approaches were enhanced by several advances in data collection methods which combine contextual environmental information with subject specific data into a single survey research effort. Sieber (1973) provided a most germane theoretical basis for mixing unobstrusive field research techniques with survey research methods. The Sieber approach had been pilot tested by Myers (1974) with mixed ethnic populations and by Valle (1974) with Latino (though not elderly) populations.

The study's overall approach also depended extensively on a series of methodologists who have primarily stressed the use of unobstrusive measures, including participant observation techniques as legitimate tools of social science inquiry (Webb et al., 1966; Campbell and Stanley, 1967; Loftland, 1966; and Truzzi, 1974). These theorists highlight the need to include the historical origins or what Blumer (1969:17) calls the "common established meanings" of the data in any analysis of social facts. This latter point was particularly useful in exploring what Romano (1969) terms the intellectual presence of the Latino and what Alverez (1971) calls the psychohistorical context.

From the gerontological perspective, Clark and Anderson (1967) and Clark (1967) were seen as having pioneered the introduction of more anthropological methodologies into the survey research arena within United States' populations. Kiefer (1971) and Moore (1971) with her notion of "situational factors" were seen as following this same theme. Both of these authors argue strongly for inclusion of the social-environmental circumstances of the elderly in any study undertaken of such groups. Prior to the San Diego study, the Andrus Gerontological Center had also undertaken research along a wide front which incorporated both anthropological and survey research techniques within a joint strategy and which had included ethnic minority populations (Bengston, 1974). On the overall issue of methodology in gerontological research, Miller (1975) proposes that, in effect the reliable approaches are numerous. It is up to the researcher to judge the appropriateness of the method as to its relevance to the problem at hand. He suggests mixed research modes as being particularly relevant to research among the elderly.

Network sampling.

The collective force of these converging influences, along with previously noted recommendations of Latino researchers (Section I), led to the research decision to enter the Latino study population in as natural a manner as possible. This, in turn, led to the elaboration of the concept of network sampling.

As indicated, a core notion of the study was to avoid imposing artificial order into the universe of population under study and rather to tap into their normal communal patterns. To proceed in this fashion requires a much more precise knowledge on the part of the researcher about the habitats, historical presence and communal-interactional conditions of the groups under study. In essence, sampling procedures need to exceed the simple numerical aggregation of the populations as presented in census data.

The notion of network subject selection stems from two principal empirically observable factors. The first of these is that the emotive capacity of human beings exceeds numerical annotation. The second is that patterns of communication/interaction between individuals and between groups of individuals are also not numerically random. Each human cohort has its own interaction/communication pattern which must be taken into account in any attempted sampling of such populations. A key consideration of network sampling is that it facilitates mapping the human territory being studied. This mapping is seen as a prelude to other types of field research, utilizing other sampling techniques. By design it draws together the social system parameters of the group or cohort under study.

It must be stressed that such sampling techniques are dependent upon a series of preparatory steps or methodological preconditions. These include the following items.

1. The researchers must be knowledgeable about the general demographic, geographic and socioeconomic features of the study area. In most instances, this information is available in documents from a variety of governmental planning and research units, as well as from the human service delivery sector. This knowledge must extend also to experiential familiarity with the study arena. Such familiarity can be acquired through a variety of techniques to include drive-through and walk-through experiences as well as the use of locality wise consultant informants.

2. The researchers must obtain sanction to enter the study area and the study groups' (in this instance, the Latino community's) social environment. This step follows what Sieber (1973:134) has outlined as obtaining legitimation for the survey and what Sotomayor (1975:159) has specifically termed obtaining "cultural sanction". To a considerable extent, this translates into linking up with a broad range of community consultants and link persons on an open process basis.

3. The researchers' strategy needs to include procedures for securing local resources to serve as interviewers and guides to the actual study population.

4. Utilizing the local human resources, the researchers then need to observe the interactional systems of the elderly themselves from the "inside" vantage point of community-based organizations and the areas' key link persons. This, in turn, permits the tailoring of the network sampling strategy to criteria specifically appropriate to the local research situation. These steps also facilitate paying attention to local linguistic and interactional custom variations.

5. Dissemination agreements and an overall dissemination plan must be worked out with the participating communities prior to initiating the research effort.

The overall theory behind these preconditions is that one taps into viable and ongoing interactional processes. One also obtains corrective feedback all along the way from as many sectors of the study groups' social environment as possible before finalizing population selection and the research design. It must be stressed also that network sampling is a planned sampling technique. It is not an accidental sampling approach. The present inquiry did not attempt just to accidentally sample 218 Latino elders scattered throughout the San Diego study area.

The interview situation: theoretical considerations.

Equally careful attention was paid to the theoretical premises and preconditions which would lead to the actual interview situation. The approach selected for the San Diego study has earlier been outlined by Myers (1974), who coined the phrase "unconventional techniques." He sees the methodology as containing several key elements which include:

- Selecting interviewers who have "shared systems of relevance" with the interviewee population.
- Including community specialist colleagues and interviewers throughout all phases of instrument design, including their assuming conceptual responsibility for instrument development as well as the data analysis. The researchers also ensure that the community specialists are socialized into a shared internalized understanding of "scientific integrity."
- Providing an intensive training process for the interviewers who are fluent in the standard and nonstandard languages of their research environment, as well as those of the interviewee population (Myers, 1974:139-142).

An additional point of critical importance to interviewing minority respondents and particularly Latinos was the aspect of "personalizing" the interaction of the interview. While not speaking of minority populations per se, Stebbins' (1972) formulation of the concept of "interview as an incipient-interpersonal relationship," was seen as especially relevant to the present inquiry. As he states:

> It was posited that unless the interviewer and respondent are sufficiently attracted to each other to permit further interaction, the interview does not take place; if they are sufficiently attracted, the interview commences.

> . . . There is reason to believe that the modern interviewer is, for many people, an opening person, and that the unstructured interview has characteristics of a pleasing sociable conversation. Awareness by the two that they are being scrutinized by one another tends to pull them into an interchange. (Stebbins, 1972:176.)

The Research Design

The preceeding theoretical considerations were directly instrumental in the constitution of the research design which included five components: (1) the preparation of a composite overview of the San Diego study area; (2) the creation of a community sanction and community consultation network; (3) the actual selection and training of a corps of community interviewers; (4) the selection of a study population tailored to local conditions; (5) the design of data collection procedures to accommodate local linguistic and situational factors.

The.San Diego study area: a composite overview.

The general demographic profile of the San Diego elderly community with particular emphasis on the cross-cultural ethnic and Latino group elderly composition has been described above. (See Tables 1, 2 and 3.) From a broader planning perspective though, San Diego has a number of unique characteristics. The area has an extensive military complex which serves as a base of operations for the U.S. Navy in several capacities. The Standard Metropolitan Statistical Area (SMSA) has a highly urbanized core, but is equally highly suburban. At the same time, large portions of the county are rural and sparsely populated. For example, nineteen American Indian tribes reside in rural reservations in the SMSA. There is considerable agricultural activity in the area which employs large numbers of persons of Mexican and Pilipino backgrounds. The North County area of San Diego contains smaller cities with concentrated mixes of urban and rural populations. The San Diego SMSA has been subdivided into six statistical subunits by the Comprehensive Planning Organization. These are titled Major Statistical Areas (MSA 0 through 6).

The researchers found that they could readily use these Major Statistical Area (MSA) designations as general designators for selection of the overall cross-cultural study respondents. From the Latino study perspective, the researchers sampled in the following local areas:

- MSA 0. Contains the central city, more urbanized core of San Diego. Latino respondents were drawn from the Old Town, Downtown, North Park, Logan Heights, Southeast San Diego, Encanto and National City areas. The demographic estimates placed approximately 44.6 percent of the Latino elderly in this MSA.
- MSA 1. Contains the urban-suburban communities to the North. These areas are mesa (plateau) type areas. Respondents were primarily drawn from the Kearney Mesa area, which includes Linda Vista. This area also includes the coastal and North San Diego areas, such as Del Mar and Poway. The demographic estimates placed approximately 10.3 percent of the Latino (age 60-plus) in this MSA.
- MSA 2. Contains the South Bay area. Latino respondents were drawn from Chula Vista, Otay. The demographic data placed approximately 11.2 percent of the Latino elderly (age 60-plus) in this MSA. This area is immediately adjacent to the Mexican border.
- MSA 3. Contains the communities of Lemon Grove and Spring Valley, from which the respondents were drawn. The area also contains the communities of La Mesa, El Cajon and others which are situated slightly north and south of these two locales. The demographic data placed approximately 11.3 percent of the Latino elderly (age 60-plus) population in this MSA.
- MSA 4. Contains the area informally designated as North County. It contains the beach communities such as Solana Beach, Carlsbad and Oceanside, and the North County inland communities such as Vista and Fallbrook. The study respondents were primarily drawn from the beach communities. The demographic data placed approximately 22.2 percent of the Latino population (age 60-plus) in this MSA. The area is contiguous with Orange County and the city of San Clemente to the north.
- MSA 5. Contains the East County, more rural and mountain areas, as well as desert areas of the San Diego SMSA. It is contiguous with Imperial County to the east. The data placed approximately 0.5 percent of the Latino population

(age 60-plus) in this MSA. Because of this fact as well as available project resources, a research decision was reached to exclude this MSA from the Latino component portion of the study. It should be noted that as a region this inland desert-mountain area does have a high concentration of Latinos if one which includes Imperial County adjacent to the east. Imperial County does have the city of Calexico within its boundaries. A large Latino population resides there and services the agribusiness of Imperial Valley. The inquiry, however, was confined to the San Diego SMSA.

Figure 1 contains a summary by percent of the estimated Latino elderly population within each of the MSAs and the actual number of respondents by percent included in the study.

San Diego fits the pattern of what Schmidt (1970:58) terms "the oasis communities" of the Southwestern United States. This implies that despite its proximity to the Pacific Ocean, San Diego is a relatively dry, hilly, desert type terrain. The oasis concept further implies that people tend to cluster along main traffic arteries where water and other amenities are more readily available. Residential patterns tend to follow the situating of commercial enterprises. In San Diego, this can be seen in the stringing out of residential subcommunities along Interstate 5 and Interstate 8, which are the region's main commercial-communicational links. In fact, these date back to the founding of the California missions. Highway 5 is the northward starting point of the mission settlements. Highway 8 provided a similar expansion route eastward to the desert interior of Southern California and Arizona.

The importance of these historical and geographical features of the San Diego study area emerged at the point of interaction with the community consultants and the respondents themselves. Several of these persons were found to be quite active in perserving the oral history of the area from Mexicano/Latino perspectives. One respondent in particular had actually complied an extensive history of the Oceanside (North San Diego County) community.

In the main, local residential areas have tended to follow the clustering pattern along the trafficked routes on the mesas and in the flatter beach areas. The clustering pattern is most visible in the North County area (MSA 4). In the more central urban city and adjacent suburban areas (MSAs 0 and 1), the clustering is less evident. Here many of the settlements follow the urban sprawl pattern which is typical of most cities. At the same time it is possible to spot core areas of the separate communities through a variety of simple techniques. For example, one can drive through and distinguish neighborhoods by observing differing architectural styles. One can also spot core areas by checking out central shopping complexes serving different geographic and population groups. Some of this information can also be confirmed by monitoring such media as television, radio and newspapers (including the more localized throw-away type advertisement newspapers). This includes also monitoring media directed at specific ethnic groups. In the case of the Latino population, this includes Spanish language radio programs and such items as ethnic group directed newsletters. The study's community consultants proved to be a valuable resource in such preliminary mapping in order to locate the residential clustering of the potential Latino elderly respondents.

Through the use of these techniques the researchers were able to locate concentrations of Latino networks in five of the six MSAs. Observational data

Figure 1

Latino Elder Study Population Distribution

Major Statistical Area	Estimated Latino Elderly by $N = 14{,}890$ (percent)	Cross Cultural Study Latino Elderly $n = 218$ (percent)	Difference (percent)
MSA O	44.6	46.3	+1.7
MSA 1	9.2	10.3	+1.1
MSA 2	11.2	10.6	+0.6
MSA 3	11.3	6.8	−4.5
MSA 4	22.2	27.1	+4.9
MSA 5	0.5	(not included)	

1970
SUBREGIONAL AREAS

MSA = Major Statistical Area as designated within the San Diego Standard Metropolitan Statistical Area (SMSA) by the Comprehensive Planning Organization (COP).

confirmed demographic estimates that had placed less than 0.5 percent of the Latino population in the East County (Mountain Empire) area, MSA 5. While exploration of networks within this dispersed Latino population would have added valuable knowledge to the study, time and costs did preclude inclusion of respondents from the area.

The San Diego study area: the creation of a community network.

In addition to the previously cited sources, support for the creation of a community sanction and community consultation networks also came from Freire (1973). This theorist fosters the notion of consciously involving the recipients of interventions (research interventions included) in all phases of the activity. Montoya (1976) also supports this view.

In setting up the network, the process was left open. The university-based coordinators were responsible for extending the network so as to incorporate groups or individuals who desired access to the research effort on an ongoing basis. In actual fact this approach allowed future participation by those who could not be involved in the beginning steps of the research. As the networks were expanded throughout the course of the study more key individuals and additional localized sanctions were made possible.

It should be noted that a similar pattern of open interaction was maintained with constituencies other than the San Diego Latino and other ethnic minority study populations. This included involving other researchers in San Diego, as well as in locales outside of the area.

As experienced by the researchers, the benefits of this process were several. First, the continuous interaction facilitated the securing of the project's interviewers. Second, it facilitated an expanding access to the study subjects. Third, this feature provided the project with a built in feedback and dissemination network.

The San Diego study area: Interviewer selection and training.

The community consultation process served as the primary vehicle for obtaining the cadre of potential interviewers. The ongoing contact was such as to allow both the university-based researchers and prospective community-based interviewers to pre-screen each other. To a large extent this process attracted experienced persons who had worked either as volunteers or agency aides. Several interviewers came to the study with prior interviewing experience on other research projects. The four-month period of November 1974 through February 1975 was allotted for this purpose. As a result, when the training period began in March 1975, a preselected group of interviewers was available.

The formal training for the interviewers encompassed twenty-eight training hours. The training was conducted in several phases. The interviewers were first trained in a major session involving all the personnel in the Cross-Cultural Study on Minority Elders. Second, the interviewers were divided into their respective ethnic groups. Here, individualized concerns about language, customs and interview approaches were emphasized. The interviewers were encouraged to proceed within their own natural styles. In addition, the first two interviews per interviewer were included as part of the training process. At that point each interviewer was debriefed to reinforce the training gains, as well as to finetune the methodology.

As part of the training content, the interviewers were upgraded in terms of information and referral techniques on services and program information for the elderly. This feature of the training was a direct consequence of community consultant input. It was provided to all of the interviewers within all of the research components, not just the Latino segment of the research. This request was supported by the interviewers themselves. Several factors were cited as the rationale for having the interviewers prepare to provide some assistance in the form of information and referral linkages to existing services. The reasons included the normal cultural courtesies one would extend an older person in need, as well as the admission by the interviewers that whether such behavior was permitted or not they would simply not walk away from an older person in need.

The project coordinators welcomed such directness on the part of the community and the interviewers. By design, the training process pattern had aimed at securing this type of input. The interviewers, however, were restricted from engaging in such activity until after the interview was completed. This aspect of interviewer/respondent interaction was then monitored in the debriefing process and included in the debriefing schedule (see Appendix B). In the second year of the project, the interviewers were trained to participate in the data analysis phases of the study. The interviewers were also incorporated into the dissemination plan for the project.

Sample selection: The application of local criteria.

The process of selecting the study population of these individuals followed the several preconditions outlined above. The actual sample contained 218 individuals, age 50 or over, spread in locales throughout the Major Statistical Areas. An attempt was made to avoid overloading the study with subjects from any one specific MSA; but some slippage did occur. In North County (MSA 4) the eventual sample did exceed the Latino elderly population estimation by 4.9 percent. The study group dipped below the estimated number of Latino elderly by 4.5 percent in the MSA 3 area (see Figure 1).

The study population selection did carry an added internal restriction: no two members from the same immediate family would be included in the study. Immediate family were identified as the respondents' parents, uncles, aunts, siblings, cousins and/or children who might be eligible for the study because they met the age criterion.

The age of 50 was selected from the standpoint of the literature as well as from considerations local to the San Diego study area. Looking to the literature, Manney (1974:14) proposes a life cycle approach to consideration of aging. He sees the third cycle beginning at age 50. According to Manney, this stage is signaled by the departure of children from home, career stabilization and the onset of chronic health problems. Neugarten (1974) starts the aging cycle at age 50 with her "young-old" category. Several emperical studies of Latino elderly populations follow suit. Steglich, Cartwright and Crouch (1968) included respondents age 50 in their study. Torres-Gil (1976) reported respondents within the 50-55 age range. In addition, the community consultation process which preceded the research had indicated that some persons age 50 to 54 could be found as natural peers to older Latinos in programs throughout the San Diego study area. The exact proportion of such persons, though, could not be ascertained prior to launching the inquiry.

These criteria were communicated to the study's link persons and used by the interviewers in their own selection process. They were adhered to throughout the study.

The San Diego study areas: The tailoring of data collection procedures.

The tailoring of the data collection procedures reflected what were termed above, the "natural" and "relational" aspects of the study environment. This meant that the interview was designed to approximate the normal ways of meeting and conversing with elderly members of the respective minority communities. Overall, the interview guide was designed to be a relatively long interpersonal experience, approximately 90-180 minutes of actual interview. Moreover, it could be a pleasant relational experience for the respondent, as well as the interviewer. A first step in the process was establishing precontacts in the modes acceptable to each ethnic group. These precontacts could range from written letters to phone calls to having a cultural broker intercede for the interview. Second, while a formal interview instrument was utilized, it was designed to be used as a guide (see Appendix B). The interviewers were instructed that each of the interview guide items represented the data being sought and *not* the way to phrase the question. Reliability was seen as resting on the interviewers' capability to tailor the interview guide to the language as well as dialect of the respondent. It must be recalled that in addition to Spanish, the interviews were also conducted in the Samoan, Guamanian, Japanese, Chinese, Pilipino and at times in Native American Indian languages. Furthermore, it also must be recognized that some of these language groups contain dialects. For example for Pilipino respondents the interview guide had to be made intelligible in the *Tagolog* and *Ilucano* dialects. With regard to the Latino portion of the study the interviewers had to be knowledgeable as to the subtle differences between *Mexicano* and *Puerto Riqueño* word usage as encountered in the San Diego area. It is important to note that linguists have long recognized among Latinos the existence of such variations, which have been termed *Calo* with regard to Latinos of Mexican heritage (García, 1971). *Pochismo* is another common though slang term used to describe such language variation with regard to Latino populations of Mexican heritage.

Third, during the interview itself, the field researchers were free to accept food and drink as deemed appropriate. When visiting Latino elderly of even the most modest means, it is not uncommon to be offered something to eat or drink. While it is courteous to initially protest any inconvenience to the elder, it is most rude not to partake once the items have been put before the visitor by the host or hostess. Finally, it should be noted that all of the interviewers were paid an honorarium of ten dollars. This honorarium was provided regardless of the length or completeness of the interview. By design the honorarium was not announced beforehand but given at the end of the session. The rationale for the payment to the respondents emerged at the suggestion of the community consultants who saw the ten dollars as an appropriate exchange to the interviewer for his or her time and information.

The interviewers were encouraged to remain aware of the importance of their style of address to the respondent. This was seen as a very critical ingredient of the interview. Included in this awareness was the recognition that the respondent's permission might have to be asked separately around particularly sensitive items within the interview or at the point of changing the topic of discussion.

This latter instruction related directly to a Latino approach to the notion of "informed consent." It should be noted that although the study was initiated prior to the publishing of the Department of Health, Education and Welfare human subject research guidelines *Federal Register* (1975), the informed consent procedures utilized did conform to option (c) of modified procedures (p. 11856). Within the modified procedures the written consent of the interviewee is not required. At the same time the respondents' rights to privacy and participation — including the refusal to participate — are clearly protected. The best advice of the project's community consultants and interviewers had indicated that the Latino elders' apprehension might well be increased rather than decreased by having to sign consent forms. The consultants also indicated the need to obtain the potential respondents' voluntary participation in the research. The natural solution which presented itself was to proceed within the ordinary mode of conversation used between younger individuals and elders as well as between Latinos who are strangers to each other. One simply waits for both the verbal and nonverbal clues to proceed further into the conversation (Valle, 1972, 1974).

Data was collected at all points of the interview. The interviewers were encouraged to record open-ended responses in as much detail as possible and in the language of the respondents. The interviewers also were encouraged to record any open-ended additions given around any close-ended items. For example, in the process of acquiring information pertinent to the close-ended item of date of birth, the interviewees would proceed to provide additional open-ended discussion on their early life experiences. This additional key information was then recorded by the interviewer.

The interviewers were left free to record information during the interview and/or after the interview itself, depending on the respondents' comfort in the situation, as well as depending upon the procedures as acceptable by each ethnic group. This approach was also designed to accommodate the information gathering style of the interviewer. Some were more comfortable writing during the interview, some more so immediately after. A general capability noticed early among the interviewers was their skill in retaining and reporting back oral history-type information. This was verified and tested during the training stage of the research and subsequently throughout the debriefings.

A debriefing strategy was included as a part of the overall contextual data collection process. The interviewers were debriefed according to two modes. These included debriefings on an interview-by-interview basis, as well as debriefings encompassing the interviewer's total sample. The debriefing intent was to collect additional contextual data regarding each interview and to obtain as much descriptive information about the interviewers' own techniques themselves. The debriefings were also designed to account for another variable. Often the interviewer observes or hears data which is so natural and normal and everyday to specific cultural and situational contexts, that he or she might well neglect to record this information. By design, the debriefings were to be conducted by the university-based coordinators. A debriefing schedule complete with close-ended coded items was developed and is included in Appendix B.

Both quantitative and qualitative analysis techniques were used within the study. With regard to the quantitative data, the Statistical Package for Social

Sciences (SPSS) computer program format was employed. For the purposes of the monograph level of reporting, frequency distributions and percentages were seen as the most appropriate statistical format. For any subsequent project reports which would compare intergroup variables, statistical measures including analysis of variance and factor analysis can be seen as applicable. In all instances, the quantitative analysis was to be played against the backdrop of the ethnic-environmental context in which it was obtained. The process of analysis was seen as being relatively long in duration, consuming most of the second year of the project. To facilitate such an analytic process, the interviewers were incorporated into the project during its second year as part of the data analysis team.

In line with the overall research approach, a dissemination network was constructed from the onset of the implementation of the research. One of the agreements made was that the participating organizations and groups would obtain the completed study at the point that the final reports emerged to the funding agency, namely, the Administration on Aging (AoA). Included in this agreement was the understanding that the participants in the dissemination network would also receive progress reports as issued from time to time during the course of the research. In this regard, specific data pertinent to the study's several constituencies was to be made available to organizations and to other researchers wherever and whenever feasible throughout the life of the study.

From the human service system's perspective, key individuals at the local, state, and national levels of the aging networks were also designated as recipients of both the study progress and final reports. As the grant funds did not extend into a third year, as originally projected, the dissemination mechanism was created prior to August 1976, to be activated once all reports were finalized. The coordinators of all the ethnic minority components within the cross-cultural study submitted dissemination plans which were left on file for the eventual dissemination of the final reports.

Summary of Theoretical and Design Considerations

From the Latino component standpoint, the mix of issues and concerns reviewed led to a sequenced approach to the research. The San Diego SMSA area was studied in detail as to the location of Latino populations. A relatively elaborate community network was developed. The consultive information received was helpful in several respects. The project staff received a storehouse of generally unreported linkage points and coping strategies by Latino elderly. The consultive advice tended to support suggestions by researchers that studies ought to focus on cultural strengths and the documentation of traditional values. Moreover, the advice received, significantly influenced the research design and its implementation. For instance, community consultant advice was instrumental in shaping the logic of the interview guide which aimed first to document the respondents' relational networks and secondarily to uncover their relationships with the formal services.

Figure 2 summarizes both the theoretical and design steps undertaken for the research. Whatever their apparent intricacy, the varied theoretical and design frameworks were seen as mutually supportive. Moreover, the flow of research events were found to evolve in the fashion suggested by Figure 2.

Figure 2
A Contextual Data Collection Strategy
_____

The Cross-Cultural Study on Minority Aging
Latino Component Data Collection Strategy Summarized
Theoretical and Design Considerations

1. The researchers are grounded in cross-cultural, as well as alternative research theory approaches.
2. The researchers are versed in ethnic specific (in the present instance, Latinos) research considerations.
3. The researchers are knowledgeable about the demographic, geographic, socioeconomic features of the study area.
4. The researchers obtain community/cultural sanction by means of community consultation.
5. The researchers are prepared to utilize local resources in the form of local interviewers. A selective screening process is developed.
6. The researchers adopt the network sampling strategy to include local criteria as appropriate.
7. The researchers tailor the data collection procedures to the local social environment.
8. A dissemination network is developed concurrent with the total research effort.

Overall, the research permits a variety of theoretical and community inputs to influence the research throughout its design, implementation and analysis stages.

STUDY POPULATION

The researchers use unobstrusive techniques which tend toward qualitative analysis based on:
• Observations of interviewee environmental interactions
• Open-ended responses of study population(s)
• Observations of local communal processes relevant to each ethnic group
• Observations of provider service networks in action

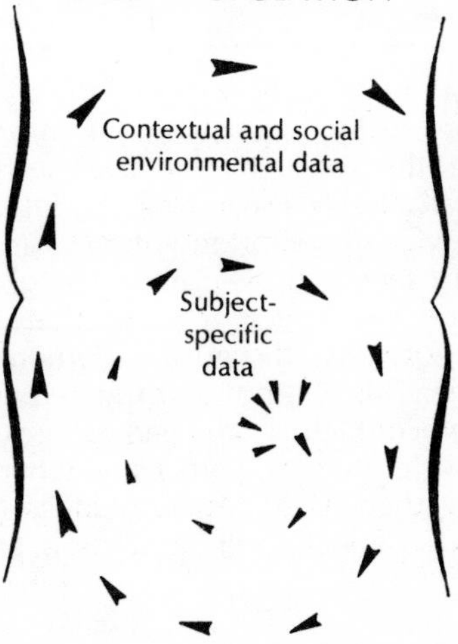

Contextual and social environmental data

Subject-specific data

The researchers employ survey research techniques which tend toward quantitative analysis based on:
• Close-ended items within the interview
• Close-ended items within the debriefing schedule

Latino networks in process

III. METHODOLOGICAL PROCEDURES

The Interview Process

The actual data-gathering process involved five activities: (1) establishing precontact, (2) travel, (3) the actual *amistad* interview, (4) recording of information, and (5) the process of debriefing. Each of these activities furnished information of use to future research efforts.

Precontact activities.

Precontacts were conducted either by phone or in person. As noted in Table 5, two-thirds (66.9 percent) of the precontacts were conducted by phone while 23.9 percent were conducted in person. In this latter instance, the interviewer would actually have a mini-interview and then set a time to return for the actual interview. In almost one-tenth of the interviews no precontacts were deemed necessary (see Table 5). It should be noted that at the point of their debriefing, the interviewers reported that 13 of the "no precontact respondents" (two-thirds), had been initially contacted by a community link person who paved the way for the interview.

Table 5
Precontact Patterns $n = 218$

Contact	f	%
By phone	146	66.9
In person	52	23.9
No precontacts	20	9.2

While a decision had been made to avoid the use of written procedures in communicating with the study population, an information sheet in Spanish providing a summary of the research objectives as well as the project's key contact persons, was available for use during the interview at the discretion of the interviewer. The interviewers reported little use of even that document with the respondents. In actual fact, it proved more useful for agency personnel and community leaders in the key target areas of the study.

It is interesting to note that the greater portion of the respondents were actually reached by phone. This was not an expected finding. The training had, in fact, stressed in-person precontacts. In the early stages the interviewers reported that phone precontacts were working, particularly when they used the name of a link person in introducing themselves. At no point in time was the authority of the university or research project itself used as a primary precontact ploy.

Travel.

By design, the research effort had obtained a strategic dispersement of interviewers for the reason of their familiarity with their locales. Also there was a need to cut down on travel distance and time. As noted in Section II, the San Diego SMSA Study Area is quite spread out. The interviewing process, therefore, required travel time by personal automobile. As reported by the interviewers, approximately one-third of the interviews could be conducted with the expenditure of a half-hour or less in round-trip travel time. The remaining two-thirds of the interviews (147 or 67.5 percent), involved over a half-hour to a full hour of travel.

The amistad interview.

In describing the interview process at the point of debriefing, the interviewers indicated they had followed the research plan. They proceeded by first engaging the respondent in conversation about other topics before moving him or her to the actual interview guide items. The debriefing information confirmed the expected pattern wherein the conversationalists, namely the interviewer and respondent, engaged in *conversational byplay* before getting down to business. As noted this byplay included focusing on light subject matter first, and serves the important purpose of allowing interviewer and respondent to test each other out and to move to more serious topics in a gradual manner. From the Latino perspective, this prelude appears to play a critical function as to whether the platica stage of conversational intimacy, as described by Valle (1972, 1974), Moore and Sánchez (1976), and Moll et al. (1976), will take place. Given this finding, a series of critical research questions emerged. How did the interviewers know when to proceed to the interview proper? How were they able to guage when to press and when to hold back with personal questioning? Could the San Diego research approach findings be systematized in some manner to have replicable research utility?

Table 6

How Did You Recognize the State of
Amistad with the Respondent? $n = 211$

Indicators		f	%
They began sharing intimate life details		108	51.2
They gave one something, e.g., food, coffee, cookies	Pre recognition	38	18.0
They began to visibly relax, smile, move closer, become more animated		28	13.2
Kept inviting me for other visits		27	12.8
Did not want me to leave	Post-recognition	5	2.4
No response		5	2.5

NOTE: Seven interviewers indicated not having reached a state of amistad with the interviewee.

9 22 75

Part of the answers to these questions emerged in the form of two concepts which had been utilized by the Latino component during the training and planning stages of the project. These were the notions of *amistad* and *confianza*. Amistad is best defined as an ambience of mutuality and friendship either situational (created at the point interview) or ongoing (based on long-standing relationships). Confianza (often used in conjunction with amistad) translates into trust and mutual confidence.

In the course of the debriefing, the interviewers were asked whether they had attained amistad. This state was reported as having been attained in almost all of the interviews, 211 (96.8 percent). More importantly, though, the researchers were interested in how the interviewers recognized the attainment of amistad. In answer, a number of clues emerged within the debriefing process. These are described in Table 6. It is perhaps important to note that in one-half of the interview situations (51.2 percent), the interviewers described recognition of the start of amistad as occurring with the respondents' beginning to share more personal and intimate details of their lives. The essence expressing more confianza in the interview situation.

More descriptively, the interviewers provided the following indicators of how they recognized attainment of amistad:

- They are eager to talk like the one who talked to me until 1:00 a.m. and kept apologizing yet he kept talking and talking.

- They've given me the fruit; *elotes* (corn), *flores* (flowers). They say, have some more coffee. They'd walk me to the car and invite me back. It was hard to break away.

- It was her posture; the way she greeted me. *Ya tenía todas sus plantas regadas* (she has just watered all her plants). I knew she was going to expect a remark on her flowers.

- *Noté que la señora L. me empezó a dar confianza. Ella empezó a hablarme en una manera muy amigable y amistosa.* (I noted that Mrs. L. began to have trust in me. She began to speak to me in a most friendly manner.)

- *Me dió nopalitos y me dió tamales.* (She gave me nopalitos and she gave me tamales.)

- I knew by the tone of her voice on the telephone, when I told her I would be on my way over after I finished my coffee. You know if a person is comfortable with you when they sit facing you and then immediately they begin showing you all their family pictures.

- *Ella y yo tuvimos una plática tan agradable que cuando menos pensamos habían pasado tres horas.* (She and I had such an agreeable plática, that without noticing it three hours had passed.)

- *Una plática como si fuera ante un amigo o un familiar. Me sentí feliz cuando me dijo: "Esta conversación contigo alivio mis penas y olvidé hasta el dolor de mi cuerpo maltratado por esta enfermedad".* (It was such a conversation as among friends or family members. I was very pleased when she told me, "In this conversation with you I've forgotten my cares and I've even forgotten the pain in my poor body from my illness".)

The interviewers reported varying lengths of time for establishing amistad ranging from just a few minutes to one instance where the interviewer was grilled by a host of the respondent's friends and neighbors who had gathered to hear the interviewer's introduction. In this instance, the interviewer recorded having reached amistad when she noted that all of the family and friends had departed one by one and she was left alone with the interviewee, who immediately began to provide personal details of her life experience in response to the interview questions.

Recording of information.

While allowance was made for individual interview styles, the debriefing period confirmed the following general patterns. First, all the interviewers followed the question flow of the interview guide from question 1 through question 54. If the respondent provided information on a latter point in an earlier response, this was noted, but the flow continued per the schedule. Second, all of the interviewers recorded a considerable amount of information during the interview proper. At the start of the research, both the university-based consultants and the interviewers had been unsure as to how writing during the interview would be received by the Latino elderly respondents. Prior discussion had proven inconclusive. Some consultants argued that it would interfere with the natural flow of the conversation while others indicated that this would be little or no problem. After completion of the first two interviews (which were part of the March 1975 training process), the latter pattern emerged as the right one. This was confirmed by the fact that all the interviewers adopted a within-the-interview recording style. Any initial hesitancy appeared on the part of the researchers and interviewer rather than the respondents. What the interviewers reported, however, is that they did not walk in and immediately begin the recording. Each would wait for the point of interview amistad to be reached before beginning to record information. Each reported also that, at the point of termination, *la despedia,* (discussed later) the recording process would stop.

Another general pattern noted during the research was the fact that all of the interviewers recorded additional information outside of the interview. This included observations made of the setting and the respondents' community situation. It also included remarks made during the initial and despedida portions of the interview when writing had not begun or had been set aside.

As a consequence of all of this recording activity, the interview guides contained a rich mix of verbatim quotes in addition to the more specific close-ended responses. It should be noted that the verbatim quotes were very often validated on the spot with the respondent, by the interviewers repeating what had been written down.

As an addendum to the process of building confianza the interviewers had been instructed to bring extra copies of the interview for the respondent if he or she wanted one. The choice of whether to give the interview guide to the respondent was left up to the discretion of the interviewer, based on the judgment of what best would facilitate the interview process. The study findings are inconclusive on this point as no clear pattern emerged within the research.

Debriefing.

As is quite possibly evident from the preceeding narrative, the debriefings served a variety of objectives. First, they were used to augment the training of the interviewers. All interviewers were debriefed after the first two interviews. Debriefing for this phase took an average of 45 minutes per interview. Second, the debriefings were used to secure reliability in the interview guide which in addition to English and several other languages was also written in standard Spanish. In turn this was modified to the colloquial Spanish during the actual interview. Third, the debriefings were used as a means of deepening the relationship between the university-based coordinators and the interviewers. Fourth, the debriefings allowed the university-based coordinators access to the individualized styles of the interviewers. Fifth, they allowed for the cross-checking of the progress of the research and the troubleshooting of any problems which arose. In this fashion, the coordinators also could correct problems emerging from faulty interviewer techniques or possible misunderstandings of the guide or its intent.

In addition to these more procedural aspects, the debriefings assisted in the collection of supplemental contextual information on the findings from the respondents. Finally, the debriefing strategy also served the critical function of gathering data on the verbal as well as nonverbal process skills of the interviewers themselves. This function had been openly shared from the start with the Latino component interviewers who actively cooperated with this research intent.

Additional Interview Findings

The use of the debriefings in the manner discussed immediately above did permit the gathering of additional information about the interview process.

The despedida, the termination ritual.

The interviewers identified still another feature of the platica interview process among the Latino elders. Frequently after the last interview guide item had been covered, and the respondent thanked and given the ten dollar honorarium, a sometimes lengthly parting conversation would ensue, termed the *despedida*, (the parting or farewell).

This interview termination process varied in length and would appear to have been situationally determined. For example, it could be shortened if the interview had to end because of the respondent's need to prepare a meal for a spouse or family members. The despedia process, though, had several notable features. For example, the conversation often would turn to mutual exchanges wherein the interviewee and interviewer would thank each other for the time spent together. It was at this point that the respondent often would show the interviewer around his or her house and garden and/or through family memorabilia. Thus, the despedida emerged as an integral closing portion to the interview of the Latino elder group. It was during this phase of the interview process that the interviewers were permitted to address the observed or expressed needs of the respondent.

A further interesting feature of the despedida was the sharing of gifts by the interviewee. This often took the form of fruits and flowers from the respondent's own garden. The respondents often expressed their willingness to be of whatever assistance they could to the interviewer. They would indicate that all the interviewer had to do was to call on them. This sharing of gifts appeared to be a normally spontaneous part of the amistad interview and followed whether or not some special assistance was provided beyond the honorarium.

Obtaining informed consent.

As a datum relevant to informed consent the interviewers did report that their conversations carried on in Spanish provided a format wherein they did need to request permission to continue with the actual interview discussion. That was particularly true when pursuing information around sensitive areas such as income and personal needs. The interviewers described gentle conversational shifts on their part, while maintaining a tone of *respeto* as discussed in the population findings, Part IV.

Interviewer/interviewee timeframe differentials.

During the course of the study several interviewers made special note of differentials in orientation to time between themselves and the respondents. One interviewer described this perceived difference in some detail:

> I had been delayed in getting to the house. I had set the appointment for 9:00 a.m., but just could not get there. I called ahead and said that I would come in the afternoon, probably around 1:00 p.m. As it was I came late, around 2:00 p.m. I was surprised to find everything waiting for me at that time. The plates for a meal had been set out and it was obvious that Senor L. and his wife had done nothing else but wait for me. I wanted to get into the interview right away, but they wouldn't hear of it. I had to eat and talk small talk. I suddenly realized that I wanted to get my job done, but these people wanted to visit and relate with me. This was what was important. I thought I really knew about all this kind of interviewing, but I sure learned how important relating is to the Mexicano. That time was not for just getting things done. This sure made me aware of how to behave in the future. (Debriefing with Martha Garcia, tape no. 3, side 3.)

Group discussions during debriefing led to the formulation of two important points related to time differentials. First, as a consequence of the group *conscientización* (critical assessment) of the above situation, the concepts of "task time" (the interviewers' orientation) and "relational time" (the respondents' orientation) emerged. The interviewers stressed that these two different orientations need to be recognized in interviewing Latino elders with special attention given to relational time aspects of the interview. The relational aspect was seen as particularly important to building of amistad within the interview. Second, the interviewers commented on the extent of planning which went into the respondents' getting ready for the relational experience of the interview. Again, since most interviews had been preceded by a precontact, most by phone, the interviewee was assumed to be in a state of readiness for the session, the circumstances that the interviewers found exceeded their expectations. Very often the house, however modest, had been thoroughly cleaned and set in order. Other appointments had been cancelled. Foods and beverages had been prepared. The interview was seen as a major event, necessitating considerable respondent input. Both of the university-based coordinators in their follow-up contacts with selected interviewees, experienced this show of courtesy and preparation to the point of being invited to remain for meals by the respondent.

Personal experience sharing by interviewers.

In the course of the debriefing process, the interviewers reported they had shared aspects of their own experiences as part of the interview process. This had not been programmed into the research effort from the beginning. The university-based coordinators became aware of the use of this technique by the interviewers through debriefing. It should be noted that the interviewers expressed clear-cut boundaries to this type of sharing. They would, for example, share information about their family or their neighborhood, or some aspect about their general life experience. However, they all made a distinct effort to avoid narrating their own personal or emotional difficulties. Admittedly, a fine line might exist between such categories but the interviewers indicated that they were sharing personal information as a means of creating confianza or amistad in the interview situation rather than burdening the respondent with their personal problems.

Provision of linking services.

The interviewers extended services to 139 (63.8 percent) of the respondents (see Table 7). These services were primarily of an informational and referral nature, but they did include a range of other activities such as translation and interpretation of documents, transportation, and advocacy on behalf of the respondents with particular agencies. In most instances, this was a one-time, short-duration service. In some instances though, the involvement of the interviewer entailed more extensive intervention. This was particularly true for such activities as assisting some respondents to verify their age and birthplace. This entailed a somewhat more lengthly process of formal correspondence with agencies, both in the United States and in Mexico. This sometimes also included follow-up contacts by the interviewer, either in person or by phone, before formal eligibility was finally verified.

Table 7
Did You Provide Services to Interviewee $n = 218$

	f	%
Yes	139	63.8
No	79	36.2

The reporting of this activity may be seen as possibly controversial from research perspectives. At the same time as was indicated in Section II, the community consultants did request that the interviewer be permitted to engage in such activity. Moreover, the interviewers did receive training in this area and had actually been provided with a services information and referral packet. At the point of debriefing, the interviewers verified that this was the normal way they behaved whenever needs were encountered, regardless of their other primary responsibilities. The interviewers also pointed out that the interviewees were receptive to their ministrations and expressed their appreciation of the service courtesies extended.

As was extressed by one of the Latino component interviewers:

> Uno tiene que auydar, en cualquier manera que se pueda, cuando uno encuentra necesidades. No se puede negar.
> (One has to help in whatever way one can when needs are encountered. One can't deny help.)

The use of community link persons.

During the debriefing the field researchers reported that in all but 5 (2.3 percent) of the interviews, they used reference link persons at either the precontact phase and/or the actual start of the interview. Some link persons actually accompanied the interviewer to introduce her or him to the respondent. The rationale provided by the field researchers for the use of the link person either by name or by actual presence centered around two key features. First, the link person gave the interviewers a degree of recognized sanction for conducting the research. Second, link persons were useful in obtaining the interest and possible cooperation of the potential respondent.

In some instances, these link persons were prominent persons active in the area of Latino aging concerns. In many other instances, they were Latino service providers of community-based agencies and known to the respondents. In still other instances, the links were other interviewees themselves who passed on word about the research project to other Latino elders known to them. In those cases where the link person actually accompanied the interviewer, he or she withdrew when the interview had progressed to the stage of obtaining personal information.

In actual practice, the link person point-of-entry approach had several variations tailored to the local situation. In the greater number of cases, the field researcher would use the name of the link person at the point of precontact. In several situations, agency personnel who served Latino elders allowed the interviewers to make presentations at their centers explaining the research effort underway and asking those present if they would volunteer to be respondents. In at least two instances, one in North County and one in the central San Diego city area, agency administrators made supportive presentations on behalf of the research effort without being asked by project staff.

Throughout the process the field researchers were instructed to use their own best judgment as to the mode of employing the link person approach. In all instances the researchers were first to obtain the permission of the link person prior to the use of his or her name.

The Logan barrio study area incident has been cited earlier (see Section I) and illustrates the issue of Latino community apprehension with research efforts. It can also serve to highlight the two key roles played by the study's community consultants and link persons. As previously described, the project interviewers were mistaken for persons operating a fraudulent insurance sign-up scheme. The research effort did have to be halted for some days until the matter could be cleared up. The community link persons were most active in both alerting the project staff as to the situation, as well as in paving the way for the researchers to return to the field. Their reassurances about the cross-cultural study expressed throughout the Logan community were the key to restarting the interviewing process.

The research project as technical assistance.

The March 1975 training process involved approximately 55 persons. This included ten university-based researchers and twenty-eight interviewers along with another project support staff to include clerical personnel. In addition, the project had entered into understandings with several ethnic minority community groups to allow some of their personnel to take part in the training as an in-kind service to the community. It so happened that some groups were undertaking their own research activities concurrent with the start of the cross-cultural study.

Other forms of in-kind technical assistance to constituencies in the community were provided throughout the life of the project. These activities included interpreting research documents and raw data for varied community-based organizations, the provision of consultive assistance at key policy meetings and the securing of additional university-based resources for groups in the community. This type of activity was performed not only by Latino component staff, but by other component personnel as well. All in all, these inputs were provided on an as-needed and as-feasible basis. In effect, the project provided a side benefit to the study community through the exchange of technical assistance.

The interviewers as analysts.

By design, during the second project year, the interviewers assisted in analyzing and interpreting the findings. At regularly scheduled meetings, interviewers were provided with the raw data and computer printouts from the 218 completed Latino study interview guides. In addition, they were given draft summaries of the monograph report at the several stages of its development. This arrangement proved mutually beneficial, both to the university-based coordinators and the interviewers. Through this means both groups were able to explore the contextual aspects of the interviews.

The interviewers were most helpful in those areas which focused on the values of the elders, their language-use patterns and the contextual meanings of the terms used. The parameters of the *servidor* system were mapped out during these sessions. In fact, the interviewers were particularly influential in determining the correct terminology, as well as the patterns of interactions within the system (see Table 31).

From the standpoint of the interviewers themselves, several reported improvement in their interviewing and outreach skills, along with their job availability. As a·group they participated in a number of major conferences on aging, for example, meetings of the Western Gerontological Association and The Fourth Annual Institute on Minority Aging held in San Diego. The Latino component interviewers also assisted in class presentations at the School of Social Work and in educational functions in other departments at San Diego State University

Combining survey and observational techniques in practice.

The joint use of survey research and observational techniques proved quite complementary in operation. The research benefits are discussed below at greater length in terms of specific findings emerging from the Latino study population. Combined methods were particularly useful in documenting the complex interplay of elements involved in the Latino respondents' critical path to services and for tracking the servidor system as described in Part IV (see Figure 3).

The interviewers themselves commented variously on the benefits to be obtained from having specific information on individual respondents while at the same time being able to document the overall situation of the respondent. From the coordinators' perspective, evident gains in the joint use of both modalities were observed on the part of the interviewers. Their natural observational skills were augmented, while at the same time they increased their capabiltiy to perceive the Latino elders' situation in more quantitative and aggregate terms.

IV. THE METHODOLOGY: ANALYSIS AND CONCLUSIONS

The Plática Methodology

The research approach has been termed the *plática* methodology from the Spanish verb meaning to converse in a friendly, intimate and mutualistic manner. The methodology was constructed from a variety of distinct but complementary elements. First, the processes of interviewer screening, selection, intensive training and debriefing were all geared toward reinforcing the interviewers' culturally synchronized information gathering skills while at the same time infusing technical research competence. In this context the reliability of the research instrument was seen as centered on the interviewers' capability to meld the interview guide into the correct local idiom. Second, the research was grounded on the premise that generation of a state of mutual trust (amistad y confianza) would be a key to a successful interview situation. Third, the project made use of link persons in order to obtain sanctioned access to the interviewee in his or her social environment. These link persons emerged at all phases of the research, but were initially located among those community persons who had responded to the first notices of the proposed research during 1973-1974, before the project was actually funded and had remained in contact with the researchers at the point when the project was launched. Finally, the research accepted the premise that the experience might be positive for the Latino elder in the context of a meaningful transaction between *personas simpáticas* (compatible individuals).

Analysis of the overall plática process indicates that the methodology can be described in terms of three distinct phases and several identifiable supportive mechanisms as outlined in Table 8.

Augmenting the Plática Methodology

As the study progressed, the researchers were able to further assess the methodological skills of the interviewers in utilizing the plática approach. A series of refinements put into action by the interviewers became evident. These clustered around two interviewer capabilities which were culturally analytical in

Table 8
The Plática Methodology in Outline

1. **Pre-Interview Phase**
   1.1 Pre-planning study of community environment is undertaken to include preliminary locating of link person networks, along with sociodemographic features of the study area.
   1.2 Community involvement activities are initiated, including formal meetings with varied constituencies and interested groups.
   1.3 Link person networks are formalized and constituency sanction for entry to the study community is secured.
   1.4 Pre-screening and selection of interviewers is undertaken, attention is paid to use of local resource personnel.
   1.5 Research instruments are tailored to the local social environment. The instruments include both unobtrusive and survey research techniques.
   1.6 Interviewers are trained for retention of natural style and incorporation of research techniques. Link persons and community-based agency personnel also may opt to participate in the training.
   1.7 The research instruments are pilot tested and finalized.

2. **Data Gathering Phase**
   2.1 *La entrada* (engaging the interviewee). This portion of phase 2 will include a precontact activity, and at all points this includes utilization of the link persons, either by having preceded or accompanying the interviewers or by obtaining their permission to use their names in obtaining an introduction to the potential respondent. This portion of phase 2 will also include the relational preliminaries prior to engaging in the formal interview itself, using the interview guide or schedule.
   2.2 The *amistad* interview (the interview proper). This portion of phase 2 will include maintaining a data gathering approach which is tuned to the culturally appropriate verbal and non-verbal behaviors which indicate when it is appropriate to proceed through the successive sensitive areas of the interview.
   2.3 *La despedia* (disengaging from the interviewee). This portion of phase 2 includes observance of culturally appropriate parting rituals including partaking of food, modest gifts, provision of services and mutual assurances. It may well happen that additional key contextual data will flood the interactive process at this point.

3. **Post Interview Phase**
   3.1 Data is assembled in terms of the several data collection instruments, to include the interview guide and the debriefing instruments.
   3.2 The interviewers are incorporated as analysts of the information gathered. The contextual analysis approach is utilized as in Figure 2.
   3.3 Initial community involvement strategies are reactivated in order to finalize the dissemination process and network prior to the termination of the funded life of the research.

4. **The Plática Supportive Mechanisms**
   4.1 Culturally syntonic (appropriate and harmonious) techniques and strategies are maintained throughout.
   4.2 Personal experience sharing is permitted, though limited to illustrations of instances where interviewer has had experiences similar to the respondent. Sharing can include one's familial status and cultural origins.
   4.3 Capability to provide basic services such as information and referral are included. Service provision, however, is seen as limited to time and resources available to the interviewer.
   4.4 Feasible technical assistance activities are maintained with the various constituencies impacting the study.
   4.5 Budget is allocated so as to provide a meaningful gift or honorarium to the respondent for the time he/she expended to assist the research by providing data.
   4.6 Provision for travel, recording and debriefing time are incorporated as integral parts of the research approach.

nature and which were more distinctly interactional in scope. This added dimension of the research is summarized in Figure 3: Cross-Cultural Augmentation of the Plática Methodology.

First, in addition to competency in the plática approach, the university-based researchers noted that the interviewers had a distinct ability to incorporate contradictory information from the respondents into a holistic profile of the Latino elder. For example, in the course of the interview the Latino elder would often express a strong desire to be independent. At the same time, he or she would describe himself or herself as turning to family and friends at times of crises. The interviewers' augmented skill came in assembling both features of the data, rather than deleting contradictory elements.

Second, the researchers noted that the interviewers were able to apply more abstract cultural concepts to the phenomena they observed and recorded. For example, they readily identified the respondents' streak of independence as under the Latino notion of *orgullo* (pride and self-dependence). The interviewers were equally conversant with such concepts as *respeto* (respect) and *dignidad* which were frequently used by the respondents. They would often clarify these concepts with appropriate examples or *dichos* (proverbs and sayings in Spanish).

Third, the researchers noted that the interviewers were themselves either active members of natural helping networks or had ready access to such systems and processes.

Fourth, the researchers further noted that the interviewers maintained a high level capability to use appropriate Latino sociability and interactional techniques. These techniques were both verbal—for example, knowing the proper forms of courteous address in Spanish—and nonverbal—knowing how to wait to be invited to sit or when to show affection to the respondent. These interactional data are retained in the study's debriefing tapes.

It should be made clear that these augmentation features are not viewed as separate from the plática methodology described in Table 8. Rather, they are viewed as more discrete aspects of the methodology which emerged from analysis of the information gathering techniques used within the Latino ambience. Moreover, these four elements were usually seen operating together as part of a complete interaction between interviewer and respondent.

Evaluating the Research Network

The inquiry made extensive use of community-based link person networks. From an evaluative standpoint, these networks proved effective in facilitating the research effort. They permitted community access to the project and they assisted in reducing areas of potential conflict and community resistance. If a criticism were to be made of the approach, it would be that the researchers must be prepared to expend considerable time in their initial formation. Once in place though, they can be maintained through the normal observance of plática interactional norms. It is important to note possible other inefficiencies, for example the fact that the openness of the process requires the researchers to explain the project anew to latecomers into the participatory process. Originally resolved issues need to be reviewed again to acquire new sanction. As this process is interactional in nature, no clear-cut rule of thumb emerges in terms of

Figure 3
Cross-Cultural Augmentation of the Platica Methodology

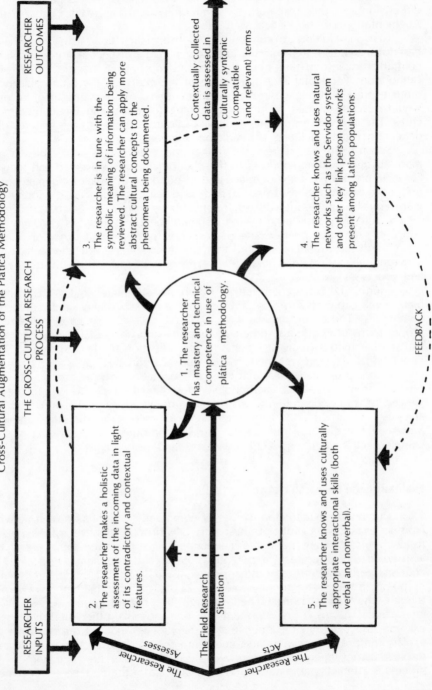

/R. Valle & L. Mendoza|

actual time expenditures. Records available on the early process of the project indicate that in the six-month period from September 1974 to February 1975, the project coordinators expended approximately eight person-hours each, or approximately one person-day per month in initiating and maintaining the community research network. This slackened through the period March 1975 to March 1976, when the project turned from data collection to data analysis. The pace of interaction with the community during the final six months of the project did pick up again to approximately four person-hours per month expended by each project coordinator in feedback to the community networks. In short, to implement effectively the study, the project administrators had to concern themselves with allocating time in order to service the research networks.

It should be noted that allocation of budget and workload resources readily can be accommodated to facilitate various peaks in network activity so as not to overburden the research system at any one point. It must be admitted that the present research did not totally preplan all of its network involvements and did overload all staff. This occurred primarily at the point that interviewer training began in March 1975. At that point, many features of the study came due. These included the need for continual interaction with the link person networks to assure selection of appropriate interviewers while at the same time beginning the respondent selection process using the network sampling techniques. Previous experience with the process could have prevented this occurrence. One simple technique later used with the research network was to announce when absences might occur on the part of the researchers because of the press of other project activities. This type of communication was successfully made at the points that data collection began and during the second project year while the data was being analyzed. The various segments of the research networks were informed that the researchers were withdrawing for a time and would reappear in community meetings in the spring of 1976. This was generally well received, not only by the Latino component link persons but by the community networks associated with the other cross-cultural study components.

The research network was a distinct asset from still another standpoint. It placed the research project squarely in the social environment. Other researchers have made note of similar benefits to be accrued from the community networks: Sotomayor (1973:50); Cuellar (1974:9); Torres-Gil (1976:112); Steglich, Cartwright and Crouch (1968:15); and Officer (1964:221) who reports explicitly on the usage of prominent Latino (Mexican American) leaders to relay information to the community. To a large extent, these commentators describe the use of networks primarily at the point of entry to the study community. At the same time, these studies contain implicit recognition verified in the San Diego study that the networks assist in maintaining the research presence in the study area over the long term.

In addition to these networks initiated by the project personnel themselves, the interviewers reported their acceptance into networks encountered in the respondents' home territory. In some instances the respondents themselves assisted in opening other doors. Moreover, as reported, the interviewers found themselves counter-interrogated by the residents of specific neighborhoods who were either passing by or who had observed the actions of the interviewers. While it could not be entirely verified within the present study, it did appear that these persons passed on the intent of the research by word of mouth.

The research networks served one additional function. Through them the project coordinators were able to actively monitor the progress of the interviewers and the research as a whole through a given locality. The link persons assisted the university-based researchers to take ongoing readings of the community ambience much as they had prior to the study's actual presence in the field. The most graphic use of this monitoring has been described previously with regard to the Logan barrio incident.

Aspects of Quality Control

From an evaluative standpoint four features of the research design were seen as ensuring quality control. These included four elements of the methodology: (1) the care paid to the selection process, (2) the care paid to the design and implementation of the training process (particularly in terms of including all project staff both university- and community-based within a single training format), (3) the pre-planning and follow-through attention paid to the debriefing process, and (4) the use of the interviewers in the analysis of the data. No one feature alone was seen as predominantly assuring reliability, but the collectivity of procedural steps used at the appropriate phase of the research did provide for constant feedback to the implementation of the methodology.

One illustration of the application of the quality control concept at the point of the debriefing process might serve to highlight the notion. In the course of the research, the interviewers encountered 25 (11.5 percent) of the respondents actually extending a wide variety of services to other persons. (This is reported in Part III in the discussion on the servidor system.) These individuals had been identified as distinct from the other interviewees and had been so noted by the university-based coordinators. During the analysis phase of the research, the interviewers were provided with their completed interviews and asked if any individuals in the project met the characteristics of what then had been termed the servidor system. The interviews each identified the servidores in their subsample. Their collective selection of 25 matched exactly those persons who had been so identified by the university-based coordinators. While this process could not meet all of the requirements of the double-blind judgment process, it does illustrate the self-corrective feedback process at work within the research to assure quality control within the effort as a whole.

Methodological Limitations

While there were many research gains made with regard to the methodology, a series of limitations emerged within the Latino component. First, an acurate-to-the-minute record of interview time expenditures were not properly maintained. As a result time estimates for the Latino study are not as available as they are for the other study populations within the entire cross-cultural study. This factor was more the result of a breakdown in the coordinators' monitoring system rather than a reflection on the recording discipline of the interviewers. The coordinators focused on the other aspects of the interview methodology and when attention was given to exact recording of the interview time procedures, well over half of the interviews had already been conducted. As a result it was difficult to obtain time estimates during the debriefings except in terms of general time block indicators such as 1-30 minute increments. The data were therefore too "loose" to record exactly. As a consequence, there is an information loss with regard to implementing the research within the Latino group. As a rough estimate, the average longer Latino component interview took 4.5 hours, the shorter took approximately 3.5 hours. Both of these estimates include all aspects of data gathering and recording, but this remains an imprecise finding.

Another limitation recognized from the start of the research was the fact that the present inquiry was a pilot test and had to be validated by future studies. In this regard, it was expected that some of the features described herein may change in their configuration in future applications.

As has been suggested in earlier parts of the narrative, the research did not proceed in an orderly manner in all of its parts. For example, the Latino linkage networks in the eastern portion of the study community, MSA 3, were not activated or utilized fully. The demographic estimates had placed 11.3 percent of the Latino elderly population in that region of the San Diego SMSA. The study only drew 6.8 percent of its respondents from this area (see Figure 1). This failing can be traced to the coordinators' not following up with a key link person in the El Cajon community who had been selected to assist with the project by other Latino network personnel. This occurred in the early stages of the research and the missed opportunity could not be recouped once the study entered the field.

Overall Outcomes

Despite the previously noted limitations, the research did attain a number of discernible outcomes. The products of the research could be outlined as follows: (1) the project did provide for a ready feedback linkage mechanism between the university and key constituencies throughout its funded life; (2) the project did provide for a built-in dissemination network which has extended beyond the funded life of the study; (3) the project did demonstrate that budget could be allocated to incorporate the natural research talent of the community with the technical research expertise of the university; (4) the methodological design did permit the capturing of quantifiable data in its native ambience complete with the contradictions and ambivalences as experienced by the Latino elder; (5) the systematic unfolding of the methodology allowed an orderly documentation of the steps taken to its implementation; (6) the overall theoretical framework employed as a rationale for the study proved on target with regard to the Latino mode of interaction; and (7) the varied social science concepts assembled for the research proved mutually compatible in terms of the actual implementation of the study.

V. STUDY POPULATION FINDINGS

A Profile of the Latino Elders

Age, sex and marital status

The Latino study population included a total of 218 individuals. The mean age for the total group was 68.1 years, the median was 67 years. With regard to age range, the youngest respondent was 52 years and the oldest was 95 years. Within the study population, 146 (67 percent) were female, 72 (33 percent) were male. Within the study group, 52.3 percent indicated they were married, 29.8 percent stated they were widowed and 12.4 percent stated they were separated or divorced.

Employment and income.

The average income for the group as a whole was $345 per month, with $225 as the median. With regard to sources of income, 60.6 percent of the respondents reported Social Security as their principal source of income. Another 7.3 percent reported they were on welfare and an additional 9.2 percent stated that they were receiving pensions, while 13.3 percent of the sample indicated that they were receiving wages and salaries. Only 1.8 percent of the respondents indicated that they were totally dependent upon family for their sustenance. Table 9 summarizes the Latino study group income information.

It should be noted that the employment findings with regard to the Latino population were inconclusive. This was particularly true with respect to the employment histories of the respondents.

Table   9

Sources of Income $n = 218$

Sources	f	%
Social Security	132	60.6
Wages, salaries	29	13.3
Pensions	20	9.2
Dept. of Welfare	16	7.3
Disability insurance	9	4.1
Unemployment benefit	1	0.5
Income from rentors/boarders	4	1.8
Family	4	1.8
No response	3	1.4

Educational levels.

Within the study group, the mean for length of formal education was 5.8 years; 50 (23.1 percent) of the subjects reported never having gone to school. The total range of formal education did extend to 20 years of schooling, with 4.4 years as the median.

Housing.

Of the Latino study group, 100 (45.8 percent) were homeowners. The remaining 118 (54.1 percent) were rentors. The rentors included 20 (9.2 percent) who were living with relatives and not directly contributing to their own housing costs.

With regard to housing costs, 72 (33 percent) of the respondents reported no housing costs due to their having paid their mortgages. This finding might have been slightly erroneous in that these respondents would still have property taxes which would translate into a form of hidden housing costs. It would appear that the 20 (9.2 percent) of the respondent group who were living with relatives were the only interviewees without any housing costs.

Overall, an overwhelming number (90.8 percent) of the respondents were living independently, either with their spouses or as widowed or single heads of households. It is perhaps important to note that within those 20 respondents who were living with relatives (primarily children), 10 indicated in some way that they would prefer to live independently. Only 10 respondents (4.5 percent) of the total study group expressed satisfaction in living as dependents in the homes of immediate kin.

Origins.

Two principal Latino groups were included within the study. Persons of Mexican heritage numbered 192 and accounted for 88.1 percent of the sample. Persons of Puerto Rican heritage number 22 and accounted for 10.1 percent of the study group. Only 4 persons (1.8 percent) of the study population gave other Latin American locales as their place of birth. With the Mexican heritage subgroup (n = 192), 140 (64.2 percent) indicated they were foreign born, coming from various sectors of Mexico. The remaining 52 (23.9 percent) indicated that they were native born, coming primarily from Texas, New Mexico, Arizona and California, including San Diego itself. In effect, two-thirds (66 percent) of the study population (the 64.2 percent of the Mexican heritage respondents and the 1.8 Latino American origin respondents), were foreign born. The 22 Puerto Rican subjects were not placed in this category as they are citizens of a United States Commonwealth territory. All 22 did indicate, though, that they had been born in Puerto Rico itself. In terms of point of origin, the Department of Health, Education and Welfare cites the 1970 census as indicating that California and Illinois tend to have higher ratios of foreign born (Mexican heritage) populations than other sections of the country, including New Mexico, Colorado and even Texas (*Selected Socio-Economic Characteristics of Ethnic Minorities*, Volume 1, 1974:27). The inference drawn here is that the larger number of foreign-born elderly within the San Diego study might reflect actual population distributions in Southern California. Such statistical relationships, though, remain to be validated in future study.

Residential patterns.

Over half of the respondents, 123 (56.5 percent), indicated they had been in their present residence for six years or more. Many of these 123 respondents indicated long-time residence in their present dwelling place. By way of illustration, one-quarter of the study group (24.8 percent), had been in their present residence 20 years or more. With regard to shorter periods of residence, only one-third of the respondents, 74 (33.9 percent), reported being in their present residence from one to five years. Only 20 (9.1 percent) had less than one-year residence in their present dwelling. The relevance of this factor with regard to the present study is that the patterns observed and recorded could be said to be applicable to a population with relatively stable residential patterns. All in all, over half of the study group had relatively long tenure in their respective residential environments. Very few were in the one year or less, more transient resident, category. Table 10 summarizes the findings.

Table 10

Length of Residence in Present Dwelling n = 218

Length of years	f		%	
Less than one	20		9.1	
1 - 5	74		33.9	
6 - 10	32		14.7	
11 - 20	37	} 123	17.0	} 56.5
More than 20	54		24.8	
No data	1		0.5	

The factor of tenure in their respective social environments is reflected in other data from the study. As had been indicated, 166 (76.1 percent) of the Latino respondents had been born outside of the continental United States. This included 140 (64.2 percent) born in Mexico, 22 (10.1 percent) born in Puerto Rico and 4 (1.8 percent) born in other Latin American locales. Among these 166 respondents 113 (72.4 percent) indicated that they had been living 20 years or more within the United States' mainland. In actual fact almost the total group, 150 (96.1 percent), had resided on the mainland for eleven or more years. The significance of this data with regard to the study is that although the study population contained a large percentage (two-thirds) of foreign born, almost all of these latter had relatively long exposure to the mainland United States ambience, based on eleven or more years of residence.

Indicators of Ethnicity

In tackling the admittedly hazy area of ethnicity, the inquiry sought out two indicators: (1) language use and (2) ethnic self-identification. It should be noted that in seeking out these two indicators, the interviewers were to adopt a passive attitude toward the respondent. The interviewers were to permit discussion to flow into the language most comfortable for the respondent. They were then to record the principal language used at the end of the interview. It should be further noted, that all of the eleven interviewers were functionally bilingual. Three of the interviewers indicated that they were most comfortable in Spanish. This is to say they thought primarily in Spanish. Some preferred English more than Spanish, or at least indicated that they thought more in English than in Spanish. As a matter of practice, the language used during the interview was set in the first stages of the interview (la entrada, the entrance, see Table 8) before specific language-use items 5 to 5c in the interview guide were asked (see Appendix B).

The same approach was used with regard to ethnic identification. As discussed in Section I of this monograph as well as in Appendix B, the researchers were concerned with the issue of mislabeling of the study population, including the use of the term "Latino" adopted for the report itself. The interviewers were instructed to listen throughout the interview for the respondents' ethnic self-identification. They were to ask for an identifier term *only* if the respondent failed to provide one, or if the one provided emerged as unclear wtihin the context of the interview. In actual fact, the only place in the interview guide for recording ethnic identification was left for Section 16, Descriptive Information, Item H, to be filled in after the interview proper.

Language.

Within the Latino study group, 183 respondents (83.9 percent) reported Spanish as their first priority language. In actual fact, 192 interviews were conducted completely in Spanish. Another 16 interviews (an additional 7.3 percent), were conducted in a bilingual mode with Spanish prodominating. Only 10 interviews (4.6 percent) were conducted solely in English.

It should be noted, however, that the English language proficiency of the study group was reported in higher percentages. Of the total group 110 respondents (50.4 percent) indicated that they could get by with spoken English. The ratio was lower with regard to written English, particularly with respect to the use of forms. Only 80 respondents (36.7 percent) stated confidence in their ability to use written English. Tables 11 through 14 summarize the language preferences and proficiency profiles of the study group.

Table 11

Language Preference Profile $n = 218$

Language	f	%
Spanish	183	83.9
English	35	16.1

Table 12

Language of Interview $n = 218$

Language	f		%	
Spanish	192	} 208	88.1	} 95.4
Bilingual	16		7.3	
English	10		4.6	

Table 13

Spoken English Proficiencies $n = 218$

Can get by speaking English	f	%
Yes	110	50.4
Yes, but w/difficulty	42	19.3
No	66	30.3

Table 14

Written English Proficiencies $n = 218$

Can get by with written forms in English	f	%
Yes	80	36.7
Yes, but w/difficulty	30	13.8
No	108	49.5

In terms of Spanish language use patterns, the Bureau of Census reports Spanish as the language of use by 71.9 percent of the 55 to 64 age group and 85.4 percent by the age 65 and over group (*Bureau of Census*, P.20, No. 250, 1973:3). With regard to Spanish language preference, Steglich and Cartwright and Crouch (1968:64) report that their Mexican heritage study group, median age 61.4 years, almost exclusively preferred Spanish even though almost 75 percent had been born in the continental United States. Torres-Gil (1976:126) reports Spanish language use and preference patterns even where apparently half knew English. Gómez, Martin and Cartwright (1973:10-11) earlier reported similar trends.

Self-identification.

As noted a total of 192 (88.1 percent) of the respondents were of Mexican heritage. Of this group 175 (80.2 percent) identified themselves as *Mexicano*. Only 10 (4.6 percent) identified as Mexican American. Another 22 (10.1 percent) explicitly declared themselves to be *Puerto Riqueños*. Still another 11 (5 percent) used a variety of self-identifiers. Some of these were based on country of origin. These included such terms as *soy Chileno, Columbiano,* or *Costa Riqueño*, etc. (I am Chileno, Columbian, Costa Rican, etc.). Others within this subgroup used a self-identifier which indicated either a cultural or ethnic heritage mix: *soy Ruso Mexicano* or *Indio Mexicano* (I am Russian Mexican or Indian Mexican). Only two of the respondents utilized a very general self-designator such as *soy ciudadano de los estados unidos* (I am a citizen of the United States). Table 15 summarizes the ethnic self-identification findings.

Table   15

Ethnic Self-Identification n = 218

Designation	f	%
Mexicano	175	80.2
Mexican American	10	4.6
Puerto Riqueño	22	10.1
Other (includes four Latinos by country of origin)	11	5.1

Other gerontologists studying elders of Mexican heritage have found a decided trend toward self-identification as Mexicano. Sotomayor (1975:131) whose study group was 92.3 percent native born, (n = 38, only 3 had been born in Mexico) termed themselves Mexicanos. Torres-Gil (1976:109-110) reported a similar finding.

The research strategy and self-identification

As described previously the research design was not only interested in the actual ethnic self-identifier used but also in whether this identifier would emerge in the interview situation. The importance of this feature of the research was seen as directly related to the labeling differentials which are present in census data. As indicated in Table 16, in slightly over three-quarters of the cases, 169 (77.5 percent) of the respondents, the ethnic designation emerged within the context of the interview itself. As a general finding these respondents would utilize some phrase such as *nosotros los Mexicanos* (we Mexicans), one or more times in the course of their conversation with the interviewers. This type of self-identification usually occurred early in the interview with regard to information item number 1, wherein the interviewee was asked:

¿ *Por favor, me puede decir donde nació?*

(Can you please tell me where you were born?)

These types of responses were often reinforced at later stages of the interview, particularly around category 15 "Cultural Values" questions 53-59. Such phrases as *yo soy Mexicano porque mi padre era Mexicano* (I am Mexican because my father was Mexican) or *Negar ser Mexicano es como pisotear a sus propios padres* (To deny being Mexican is like kicking aside one's parents), were typical of the statements made by the interviewees.

Within reference to the remaining 49 (22.5 percent) of the respondents, ethnic self-identification did not emerge clearly enough within the context of the interview and had to be solicited by the interviewer. Table 16 summarizes the data.

Table   16

Obtaining of Ethnic Self-Identification

by Interviewer n = 218

Self-identification	f	%
Emerged in the context of the interview	169	77.5
Was solicited by interviewer	49	22.5

Expressed Needs

The respondents experienced a variety of needs. The scatter is summarized in Table 17. This scatter was based on the first priority response to item 14 which asked the respondent to identify his or her principal problem(s) or need(s) on the basis of priority.

Table 17

What Presently Causes You the Greatest Concern

n = 218

Item of Concern	f	%
Health	78	35.8
Transportation	26	11.9
Personal problems (mostly concerns about children)	24	11.0
Income	14	6.4
Language	8	3.7
Age	7	3.2
Legal	1	0.5
Other (need for companionship expressed variously)	21	9.6
No response	39	17.9

The literature on Latino elderly expresses a similar scatter in terms of expressed need. Steglich, Cartwright and Crouch (1968:38) report health as the priority need within their study population, n = 291. Sotomayor (1973:101) reported the greatest concerns of her study population as illness, being forgotten and loneliness. Torres-Gil (1976:156) indicated lack of money, inadequate transportation and health as major areas of concern within his study population.

Within the study the interviewers had been instructed to probe the needs responses in depth. It was here that another pattern in describing needs began to emerge. The health area serves to illustrate the circumstances encountered.

Health.

Only slightly over one-third of the Latino study group, 78 respondents (35.8 percent), declared health as a priority concern. Yet, when pressed further, less than one-third, 67 (30.7 percent), stated outright that they saw their present health status as good. Of the remaining respondents, 66 (30.3 percent), described their health as faír and more than one-third, 85 (39.0 percent), described themselves in poor health (see Table 18).

It is interesting to note, though, that even those 30.7 percent describing their health as "good" qualified their statements within the open-ended discussion process of the plática interview. Three qualitatively different versions of "good health" emerged about evenly divided within this subsample of 67 respondents. One portion of the subgroup indicated that they accepted health problems as a part of being older. As one such respondent stated: *He tenido mis problemas de salud pero no los considero problemas de incapacidad,* (I have had my health problems, but I don't consider them incapacitating). In effect these respondents saw their health as good, given other more problemmatical circumstances. A second subgroup included those who had been recently very ill, and in some instances hospitalized for major surgery but who were now recovered and described their health as "good." A third subgroup of approximately 20 respondents indicated in some fashion that they did, in effect, feel good now or had never felt better in their lives. One respondent in this last subcategory, age 67, was explicit enough to indicate that he felt as good now as he had at the age of 17. As can be noted in Table 19, 131 (60 percent) of the study population had actually used health services or recently been inpatients in hospitals and/or convalescent facilities.

Table   18

Health Status

(Respondent Self-Description)

n = 218

Status	f	%
Good	67	30.7
Fair	66	30.3
Poor	85	39.0

Table   19

Latino Elder Health Facility Use   n = 218

Has used health services	f	%
Yes	131	60
No	87	40

Transportation.

When asked in a close-ended manner (interview guide item 34) if transportation was available at the point of need 185 (84.8 percent) of the respondents said "Yes." As with the health area, a different pattern began to emerge within the open-ended aspects of the plática interview. As asked in the interview, the transportation question was associated with transportation around crisis or emergencies, but as the interview progressed the respondent group indicated that they did not have the ready means for transportation for the day-to-day needs such as shopping, visiting family and friends, and for recreation.

In terms of mode of transportation, the auto was singled out as the primary means of transportation by 119 (54.6 percent) of the respondents. Yet only 58 (26.6 percent) owned their own auto. Public transportation was the next highest primary means of transportation used by 72 (33 percent) of the interviewees. With reference to the San Diego area, this trend coincided with an earlier study with a much larger elderly (though not minority) study group. Kaplan in his 1973 survey of 500 residents of the area, age 65 or more, found that 31 percent had used public transportation thirty days prior to being interviewed (1973:1) He found though, that more than half (52 percent) had a valid California drivers license and all but 1 percent of this subgroup had access to automobiles.

Nutrition.

Three-quarters of the respondents reported reliance on Latino ethnic foods or a mix of Latino ethnic foods for at least one meal during the day. A portion of the 47 respondents (21.6 percent) indicated that they relied on non-Latino ethnic foods for their dietary needs.

Within the sample 189 (86.7 percent) reported preparing their own meals or having their spouses prepare their meals for them. Only 15 respondents (6.9 percent) indicated that a friend or neighbor prepared their meals, while an additional 4 respondents (1.8 percent) indicated dependency on a housekeeper. Only 3 (1.3 percent) of the total study group reported relying on a nutrition center or service such as Meals on Wheels for their dietary needs.

A little over half of the respondents, 126 (57.8 percent), indicated that they ate their meals with others, primarily relatives, although in a few instances friends were named as eating companions. Congregate meals did not feature within the study group. Another 88 (40.3 percent) of the respondents indicated that they ate their meals alone. When asked what could improve their meals or overall nutrition, almost two-thirds of the respondents, 134 (61.5 percent), did not respond with any suggestions. At the same time, the interviewers observed and reported that respondents did encounter nutritional problems in terms of lack of financial resources at the end of the month. Meals were being skipped because the check did not stretch to the end of the month, particularly if the respondent had encountered some extra expense elsewhere during the month. The interviewers indicated certain sensitivity and reserve on the part of the respondents around the questions on nutrition—at times bordering on unwillingness to discuss the area at all.

Further inconsistencies around the area of needs.

The interviewers encountered a further series of qualifying attitudes with regard to the respondents' documentation of their own needs. The interviewers noted in particular, considerable hesitancy on the part of the respondents when talking about their own needs. Many respondents couched the whole area of their expressed needs and of use of programs serving those needs in the language describing persons other than themselves. For example, with regard to obtaining income assistance or food stamps, a common refrain was:

Si, pero esas (asistencia o estampillas) son para otros más pobres que nosotros.
(Oh yes, but these (welfare or food stamps) are for others who are poorer than ourselves.)

Yet many of the interviewees who, for example, had reported themselves not financially pressed would often remark on how difficult it was to get to the end of the month. This was always brought up later and discussed indirectly in the latter stages of the interview. In this way information surfaced that 60 percent of the interviewees had utilized health services or been inpatients in a hospital (see Table 18). It was in this manner that many chronic, and at times incapacitating, health problems were reported. However, in almost the same breath that the health difficulty was noted, the respondents would express the idea that these circumstances had to be endured or that one had to be grateful for whatever health one had. The notion of suffering and enduring was commonly connected with the difficulties or adversities mentioned. This attitude was captured by one 69-year-old respondent who had endured years of use of a mobile breathing apparatus, resulting from a lung-disabling disease earlier in life.

Bueno, uno tiene que sufrir lo que venga en la vida, pero uno tiene que seguir andando.

(Well, one has to endure what comes in life, but one has to go on.)

Orientation Toward Services

An important objective of the study was to obtain information on the respondents' patterns of interaction with the formal networks of services. Information was sought in three principal areas, namely the Latino respondents' knowledge, use of, and recommendations about the human services.

Knowledge of services.

When asked directly if they knew of any agencies or types of services, two-thirds of the study population, 144 (66.1 percent), answered yes. The remaining one-third, 77 (33.9 percent), of the interviewees responded that they did not know of any agency or services. When the question of services was pursued further though, many of this latter one-third did indicate knowing of specific programs such as Medicare and MediCal or in some instances staff of agencies who worked on an outreach basis in the community.

Knowledge about health insurance programs did prevail within the study group. An overwhelming 88.5 percent (193) of the respondents indicated they knew about Medicare, and 187 (85.8 percent) knew about MediCal (see Table 20).

Table 20
Knowledge of Health Programs $n = 218$

Question/response	f	%
1. Know about MediCal?		
Yes	187	85.8
No	30	13.7
No data	1	0.5
2. Know about Medicare?		
Yes	193	88.5
No	24	11.0
No data	1	0.5

The literature points to similar patterns in other groups of Latino elderly studied. Sotomayor (1973:137-138) indicates that even though there were a number of services within walking distance of the respondents in her sample, many indicated a lack of knowledge, or as she states, they had a reluctance to acknowledge them—yet reference is made to the fact that a substantial portion were active cases within the Denver, Colorado, Department of Public Welfare. Cuellar (1974:14-15) reports that professional and paraprofessional services were provided for seniors at the housing project where they resided, yet with the exception of 2 people out of 105, the professional service provider was not considered as a member of their emergency network. In Steglich, Cartwright and Crouch's study (1968:56) there was a limited knowledge of programs designed to aid older persons. Of the total sample only 57 percent knew of just one program—Social Security.

Use of services.

When pressed within the plática interview, however, the respondents did acknowledge using services. Over two-thirds of 152 (69.7 percent) answered affirmatively that they had used or would use services. Table 21 summarizes these responses, while Table 22 summarizes the variety of services used.

Table 21
Have Used or Would Use Agencies   *n* = 218

	f		%	
Using or have used	94	} 152	43.1	} 69.7
Would use	58		26.6	
Would not use	13		6.0	
No data	53		24.3	

Table 22
Specific Needs That Agencies Have Helped Meet   *n* = 218

Needs	*f*	%
Health-medical care	65	29.8
Financial	18	8.3
Nutrition	5	2.3
Transportation	10	4.5
Counseling/advising	5	2.3
Other (to include general community multiservice-type agency)	18	8.3
No data	97	44.5

At the same time, a curious anomaly developed with regard to the health insurances. When asked if they had used, or were using or would use MediCal, almost half of the respondent group, 108 (49.5 percent), answered in the negative. The percentage answering "no" was even higher with regard to Medicare.

At the point of debriefing, the interviewers reported the whole area of orientation to services as the more difficult portion of the interview and that health stood out as the single most sensitive area. A series of statements indicating mistrust of health care and fear of illness and health systems personnel emerged as the core concern for 127 (58.3 percent) of the respondents in the

/ **R. Valle & L. Mendoza**|

open-ended discussions surrounding this area. The basic attitude was put forth by one respondent:

> ¿Porque ir (al doctor)? Si uno va encontrar mil otras casas mal. Vienen más trastornos y cuestan más dinero.
> (Why go to the doctor? One will only find more things wrong. There will only be more trouble and it will all cost more money.)

Table 23 highlights the concerns of the respondents with regard to the health area.

Table 23

Reasons Latino Elders Hesitate to
Use Doctors or Health Services   n = 218

Reason	f	%
Language barriers	31	14.2
Financial barriers	32	14.7
Transportation	6	2.7
Mistrust of health care (also fear of illness or fear of finding out about illness)	127	58.3
No data	22	10.1

Recommendations for Service Delivery

The respondents were asked to recommend types of services needed. Transportation emerged as the principal recommendation by almost half of the respondent group, 97 (44.5 percent). At the same time, almost one-third (32.6 percent) had no recommendations to offer (see Table 24).

Table 24

Service Delivery Recommendations   n = 218

Types of services*	f	%
Bilingual services	8	3.7
More transportation	97	44.5
Outreach	27	12.4
Jobs	11	5.0
Other	4	1.8
No data	71	32.6

* Types of services needed but not available as known to respondents.

The "no response" percentage increased dramatically when the respondents were asked to make recommendations with regard to capabilities needed by agency personnel. Here, 163 (74.8 percent), or three-quarters of the study group had no recommendations to make (see Table 25).

Table 25

Capabilities Needed by Agency Personnel   n = 218

Capability	f	%
Bilingual	40	18.3
Cultural	12	5.5
Other (special technical knowledge)	3	1.4
No data	163	74.8

Again, the observation made by Sotomayor (1973) that the whole area of services just did not register clearly with her sample would appear to respond with the San Diego study group. At the same time, while the San Diego study located a sense of apprehension around the health area, no overt attitudes of hostility toward services were encountered in the study population. Moreover, despite all the ambivalence noted toward services 63.8 percent did accept linkage-type services as provided by the interviewers. As also indicated earlier, over two-thirds had reported actual use of some services (see Table 21).

Familial and Primary Networks

A key feature of the inquiry was the examination of the respondents' linkages and interactional patterns with familial and other primary networks. Almost the total respondent population indicated some form of family ties. Only 4 (1.8 percent) indicated that they were without any family members either within or outside of San Diego SMSA. All of the remaining 214 respondents (98.2 percent) responded having active familial networks. As can be noted in Table 26, over half of the respondents, 118 (55.1 percent), had relatives living in the same residence with them; a much larger percentage, 88.3 (189 respondents) reported kin in their immediate neighborhoods, and an almost like percentage, 83.1 (178 respondents) reported kin proximate to them in the greater San Diego area. Finally, 189 respondents (88.3 percent) reported still other family members outside of the San Diego area with whom they maintained some form of ongoing contact.

Table 26

Family Networks by Degree of Kinship and
Proximity (or Locale) of Residence   n = 214*

Category of Proximity	Brothers/ Sisters		Children		Grand- Children		Other Relatives		Totals	
	f	%	f	%	f	%	f	%	f	%
Same residence	11	5.2	69	32.2	29	13.5	9	4.2	118	55.1
Immediate neighborhood	35	16.3	76	35.5	64	30.0	14	6.5	189	88.3
San Diego County	33	15.4	67	31.3	63	29.4	15	7.0	178	83.1
Outside of San Diego area	51	23.8	59	27.6	40	18.7	39	18.2	189	88.3

* Four interviewees indicated they had no family, thus, n = 214.
NOTE: Frequencies and percentages will not equal 100 as respondents could provide multiple responses.

/ R. Valle & L. Mendoza|

With regard to frequency of contact approximately two-thirds, 141 (66 percent), of the respondents indicated either daily or weekly contacts with kin (exclusive of those kin living in their same residence). Another 40 (18.7 percent) reported monthly contacts or several times a month contacts. A portion, 28 (13 percent), reported less frequent to no contact at all with relatives. All in all, major portions of the study group (84.7 percent) indicated family ties while 13.0 percent reported little or no family interaction. Table 27 summarizes the data.

Table 27

Contact Patterns with Frequency Networks   n = 214

Contact	f	%
Daily to weekly	141	66.0
Several times monthly to monthly only	40	18.7
Less frequently to never	28	13.0
No response	5	2.3

The respondents were also asked about their contact preferences. The majority, 123 (57.5 percent), were pleased with the patterns as reported (see Table 27). A large segment of the study group though, 90 (42 percent), indicated that they wanted more frequent contact. Included in this latter number were almost the total subgroup who had reported less than monthly to no contact with primary networks (see Table 28).

Table 28

Respondent Contact Preferences   n = 214

Contact	f	%
More often	90	42.0
About the same	123	57.5
Less often	1	0.5

Use of primary networks.

Regular visiting-type contact emerged as one type of interaction with primary networks with activity centered largely on familial interaction. The respondents were asked to whom they would first turn when difficulties or crises arose. This provided a look at additional uses of their primary networks including their expansion to include friends and neighbors.

When asked about their initial response in meeting problems or crises, almost three-quarters, 153 (70.2 percent), of the respondents indicated that they would turn first to some member of their family. Another 28 (12.8 percent) of the respondents reported they would first turn to friends or neighbors. All in all, a total of 83 percent (four-fifths) of the study group turned first to their primary networks of kin or friends and neighbors as an initial step in coping with crises. Only 13 (6 percent) reported engaging professional persons or proceeding directly to agencies as an initial coping step. It is also interesting to note that almost 10 percent of the study group chose to turn to no one or to depend primarily on themselves as an initial response. Table 29 summarizes the data.

Table 29
When Difficulties Arise, To Whom Do You Go First?   n = 218

Do you go first	f	%
Family	153 } 181*	70.2 } 83.0*
Neighbor or friend	28	12.8
Professional person/ human agency or organized service group	13	6.0
Self or no one	21	9.6
No response, or uncertain, or unclear	3	1.4

* primary networks

In order to obtain a more precise delineation of the respondents' primary coping patterns, the interviewees were asked where they would first turn in cases where more specific needs arose. As noted in Table 30 the pattern of turning first to the family and friend network remained as a consistent first coping step for the respondent group, dipping only to a relative low of half of the study population (50.9 percent and 49.9 percent respectively) with regard to major financial and food needs. It is noteworthy that only with regard to illness did agency person rate first in the coping ladder. Here (illness), almost one-fifth (20.6 percent) of the Latino study group reported turning first to professionals. Another noticeable trend was the relative increase in the pattern of the respondents turning first to themselves for minor and major financial need, food and counseling or advice.

Table 30
Coping Networks Summarized by Percent   n = 218

Need	To Whom Respondents Turn		
	Family/friend/neighbor	Professional person/ human service agencies agencies or organized groups	Self or no one
Illness	70.2	20.6	7.8
Transportation	74.3	13.3	8.7
Financial help			
Minor	83.6	4.1	27.5
Major	50.9	12.9	23.4
Food	49.9	5.0	23.9
Physical help	63.3	8.7	16.5
Counseling or advice	63.8	6.4	20.6

The literature on Latinos indicates similar findings. Carp (1970:130) reports family and friends as the primary source of information for the Latino elder of

/ R. Valle & L. Mendoza|

Mexican heritage. Sotomayor (1973:96) cites a similar finding. Others writing of Latino populations in general, report similar patterns. Padilla, Carlos and Keefe (1976:18) report that 62 percent of the total sample (n = 666) responded that relatives and friends are the most common sources of help when they have emotional problems. Valle (1974:97-100) indicates that the respondents (n = 187) sought help or helped each other by sharing available resources such as goods, services or intangible personal support.

Primary level helping activity.

The techniques utilized throughout the study yielded evidence of varied types of helping activity within the respondent group itself. Overall, slightly over two-thirds of the respondents, 149 (68.3 percent), either reported or were observed to be assisting others. These respondents could be broken down into three distinct categories: (1) persons who indicated a willingness to help others, but lack the present capability to do so; (2) persons who reported assisting their neighbors with many of the day-to-day needs; and (3) persons who were encountered in extensive helping activity including brokering interaction with the formal human service networks. This latter group numbered 25 respondents scattered throughout the total San Diego study area and represented 16.8 percent of the helping networks (n = 149) or 11.5 percent of the total Latino study population (n = 218). Table 31 summarizes the helping patterns observed.

Table 31

Los Servidores: Helping/Brokering Activity by Category   n = 149

Category	f	%	Description of Helping Activity
Servidores Comunicativos* (The community service broker link person)	25	16.8	These persons were found to be engaged in helping activity, which included extensive interaction with formal and informal human service networks. (Group represented 11.5 percent of the total study population n = 218.)
Los Vecinos, Los Servidores Personales (The neighbors, the local service broker, link person)	110	73.8	These persons reported helping their neighbors on an ongoing basis but lacked awareness of interaction with formal service agencies.
Servidores Potenciales (Potential service brokers, link persons)	14	9.4	These persons indicated they had helped earlier in their lives or were presently willing to assist others but lacked the capabilities to do so because of their present circumstances, including physical incapacities. These potential servidores had either been servidores comunicativos or vecinos earlier in their lives.

* Note: The term Servidores Comunicativos was first coined by Sra. Lilia Lopez. The distinctions were further clarified between categories by Sra. Herminia Enrique. Both served as project interviewers.

As evidenced in Table 32, although minor financial assistance emerged as the modal category, the types of assistance provided by the respondents themselves varied.

Table 32

Type of Assistance Given $n = 149$

Type	f	%
Care during illness	8	5.5
Transportation	24	16.0
Financial	34	22.8
Minor *consejos* (advice, counseling)	13	8.7
Physical assistance (e.g., moving objects)	18	12.1
Food or meals	28	18.8
Other general help	24	16.1

The language of helping.

The term *servidores* was used to describe the observed helping brokering activity, and was drawn from the language used by the respondents themselves. Throughout the study, variants of the verb *servir* (to serve, assist or help) appeared constantly in a wide range of interview responses. The term was not just restricted to discussion of direct helping activity. For example in describing qualities they liked in their neighborhood, some respondents indicated that they found their neighbors *muy servicales* (very disposed to help, to be of assistance). Table 33 illustrates the term as used in several interview contexts.

Total language of helping served as an additional purpose vis-a-vis the San Diego study. It permitted the labeling of the natural helping networks of servidores as the servidor system, thereby making use of the local idiom.

Expectations of the Elderly

A dimension considered important vis-a-vis the respondents was the more open-ended element of their own expectations as to how they should be treated. Equally important within this category was the respondents' view of where responsibility for social problems and human need resolutions should rest.

Treatment of the elderly.

The respondents were relatively noncommittal when asked specifically about their expectations of agencies (see Tables 24 and 25). Throughout other portions of the interview, though, the interviewees were quite prescriptive in regard to the qualities desired in persons who would interact with Latino elders (see Table 34). To a considerable extent, these responses centered around how they themselves had been taught as youngsters to treat elders. While the responses did not lend themselves to a quantitative analysis, a certain patterned refrain was evident with regard to three specific questions. (1) How should older persons be treated when in need? (2) Why did they turn first for help to the person they had designated? (3) What qualities did they like in persons who worked with elders?

In the analysis of this part of the data a composite view of the respondents'

Table   33

Illustrations of Use of Term *Servir* Throughout Latino Study Group

Usage of term *Servir*	Spanish	English
with regard to the quality of respondent neighborhoods	Los vecinos son muy serviciales. En cualquier cosa ayudan.	My neighbors are most helpful, they help with everything.
	Todos ellos (vecinos) son agradables y *serviciales* cuando estoy necesitado.	All the neighbors are most pleasant and helpful when I am in need.
	Con union completa y sirviendose en necesidades.	A perfect relation, mutually assisting each other in need.
with regard to "values" responses	Ayudarse uno al otro. Prestandose servicio y ser uno amable.	Helping one another. Offering service and being warm and amiable.
	Cuando se ofrecia prestar servicio le *serviamos* a personas necesitadas.	When we offered to serve, we served needy persons.
with regard to relative contact patterns	Ellos tienen su vida aparte y vienen cuando se les hace posible. Uno no puede vivir visitandolos pero estamos listos para servirlos cuando sea necesario.	They have their own lives and come when it is possible. One cannot live just visiting, but we are ready to help whenever necessary.
OPENING AND TERMINATION OF INTERVIEW		
Often in answering the phone at the point of the interview precontact the respondent would answer:	Soy la Senora T., para servirle.	I am Mrs. T., allow me to be of assistance.
Often at the point of terminating the interview, when the respondent was provided his or her honorarium, he or she would exclaim:	¡Hay muchas gracias! si le puedo servir en algo, por favor llameme.	Thank you so much, if I can be any assistance to you in any way, please call me!

view was drawn. In the view of the Latino elder, he or she would desire the following:

> Queremos alguien comprensivo; que nos trate con respeto; que siempre esté dispuesto a ayudar; que sea atento y servicial; que sea gentil y paciente; que presente cortesia; que sea sociable y amable y nos trate con delicadeza y dignidad.
> (We would like someone who is understanding; who treats us with respect; who is always willing to help; who is attentive and who serves; who is gentle and patient; courteous and friendly; sociable and who treats us with refinement and dignity.)

It is significant to note that the terminology which emerged was consistently relational in focus.

Table 34
Terminology of Significant Expectations of Elders

How To Treat Elders	Qualities Valued in Person(s) First Turned to for Help	Qualities Valued in Agency People
• Con respeto: (with respect)** • Con dignidad: (with dignity) • Con delicadeza: (gentleness) • Con comprension: (understanding) • Con consideración: (consideration) • Con cariño: (affection) • Con paciencia: (patience)	• Siempre dispuestos a ayudar: (They are always ready to help) • Me quieren: (They care for me) • Son muy atentos: (They are very attentive) • Son comprensivos: (They are understanding) • Me conocen: (They know me)	• Nos trata con respeto* (He/she treats us with respect) • No nos da prisa, pero se pueda dar prisa si lo necesitas: (He or she doesn't hurry, but will hurry if there is a need to) • Todo lo que se le ofrece a uno, lo hace. Es muy complido: (Whatever he/she offers, he or she does, follows through) • Si no lo puede hacer llama a alguien quien lo haga: (If he/she cannot provide, he or she secures someone who can) • Viene a la casa. Puede ayudar fuera de la oficina: (He/she comes to the house. Can help outside the office) • Nos saluda por nombre: (He/she greets us by our name) • Uno puede llamar a cualquier hora: (One can call on him or her at any time) • Sabe ayudar con problemas: (Knows how to solve problems)

*NOTE: Terms have been arranged in relative order of frequency.
**NOTE: The term respeto was universally mentioned by the respondent group.

With regard to the expectation of respeto (respect), Sotomayor (1973:138) writes that her respondents reported that what they most wanted from the government was to be treated with respect. Earlier, Clark and Kiefer (1969:10) reported that respect was the most common term heard when inquiring about relationships with the Mexican American family.

Responsibility for problem resolution.

Another observable contrast was noted between the respondents' primary coping behavior and their recommendations as to who could best resolve key problem areas. As indicated, the respondents reported turning first for help to their networks of family and friends first when faced with a crisis. When pressed further as to who could best address the problems affecting the elderly, three-quarters of the total respondent group, 160 (73.4 percent), specified *el gobierno* (the government), as the problem solver. It is important to note that *none* of the interviewers specified the family as a possible resource for resolving the broader social problems they were discussing. In a number of instances, respondents clearly indicated that they did not want to impose on their children or did not expect either children or other family to provide for them.

Table 35

What Can Be Done To Change Present
Circumstances of the Elderly   n = 218*

Problem resolution by	f	%
Government programs	160	73.4
Take care of themselves	22	10.1
Family	0	0.0
Other	2	0.9
No response	34	15.6

This finding would appear to be supported in terms of other studies. Steglich, Cartwright and Crouch (1968:47) report that although slightly more than half of their respondents lived with children, many did not believe that children had any obligation to provide for them. Respondents indicated, rather, that problem resolution resided in the government. Sotomayor (1973:137) reports that 42 percent of her study sample indicated that economic help, better housing, jobs and transportation assistance should come from the government. Cuellar (1976:61), reporting on a study conducted through The Andrus Gerontology Center, states that 61 percent of the elder Mexicanos had no expectation of familial help if they found themselves without money. This, even though 72 percent preferred to live in the vecindad (neighborhood or barrio) as their children. Torres-Gil (1976:158) reports that his study population's expectation was that problem resolution would come through political action, some form of advocacy or the social services. The family was mentioned as a fourth possible resource.

Aspects of Life Satisfaction

The research also focused on examining the respondents' surroundings as an index of life satisfaction. While these were not cast in terms of social activities, they did provide some range of the perceptions of the respondents' social environment.

Immediate living environment.

The majority of respondents, 194 (89 percent), reported themselves as relatively well satisfied with their immediate neighborhood. Within the Latino group, this factor of neighborhood satisfaction was explored in some detail. When asked to describe their present barrio or neighborhood environments, almost three-quarters of the study group, 158 (72.5 percent) of the respondents, rated theirs as good, indicating in Spanish that they lived en una buena vecindad (a good neighborhood). Another 36 (16.5 percent) respondents gave their neighborhood a fair rating—una vecindad mediana (a moderately satisfying neighborhood). Slightly less than one-quarter, 23 (10.5 percent), of the study population, reported that they considered their neighborhood to be bad; stating that they lived in un lugar pobre ó malo (a poor or terrible neighborhood). With regard to those responses which rated their neighborhood as good or fair, no clear pattern was discernible, although "good neighbors" emerged as one modal favorable response (see Table 36).

Table 36
Ratings of Neighborhood   n = 218

Rating	f	%
Good	158	72.5
Fair	36	16.5
Poor	23	10.5
No response	1	0.5

The general satisfaction of Latino elderly with their immediate environment has been noted by other investigators. Carp (1969:463) in a Texas study sought to determine why Mexican American elderly who would qualify for public housing made no effective effort to secure it. When asked their reasons for remaining in present housing, nearly one-third said they were happy where they were and saw no reason to move. Of the study sample, 45 percent wanted to remain in homes they owned and others mentioned proximity to kin or not wanting to leave neighbors.

Another common response pattern with regard to neighbors was the notion of a peaceful or tranquil neighborhood; *esta es una vecinidad tranquila*. There was also the recurrent use of such terms as: *Nos ayudamos, los vecinos son muy servicales* (we help each other); *aqui somos como una familia* (here we are like a family); *cooperamos* (we cooperate); *prestamos servicio* (we lend each other assistance); and *compartimos* (we share), often accompanied the possitive descriptions of the neighborhoods in either the "good" or "fair" categories. It is perhaps important to note that the ethnic composition of the neighborhood was not in itself singled out as a key factor with the study group. Table 37 summarizes the principal reasons given by the respondent group to describe their "good" and "fair" positive neighborhood ratings.

Table 37
Factors Contributing to Positive Neighborhood Ratings
in the Latino Population   n = 218

Like about your neighborhood	f	%
Relational/Interactional Factors		
• Near Family	11	5.1
• People good neighbors	60	27.5
Rootedness Factors		
• Strong attachment to present home/ long-time resident	40	18.4
• Comfortable/secure/familiar surroundings	51	23.4
Ethnicity of Neighbors	4	1.8
Convenience of Location	21	9.6
Independence (likes freedom of movement in present locale)	2	0.9
No response	29	13.3

In an attempt to attain more qualitative specificity regarding neighborhood life, respondents were asked to indicate any possible negative features about their neighborhoods (see Table 38). First, in contrast to the large number of respondents commenting in positive modes, namely 194 (89 percent) of the study group, over two-thirds of the respondents, 151 (69.3 percent), had no response regarding negative neighborhood features. Second, the ethnic composition of the neighborhood, again, received relatively little mention.

Table 38

Features Contributing to Negative Neighborhood Ratings
with the Latino Population n = 218

Dislike about your neighborhood	f		%	
Don't like in general	2		0.9	
No friends	2		0.9	
No family	2		0.9	
Ethnic make-up (not enough persons of respondents' ethnicity)	5	67	2.3	30.7
Inconvenient, lack of resources	24		11.0	
Lack of security/crime factor	31		14.2	
Other (generalized negative feeling)	1		0.5	
No response	151		69.3	

The respondents were asked further that if given the opportunity would they move from their present locale. Approximately two-thirds of the study group, 142 (65.1 percent), held firm to the opinion that they could find no compelling reason to move (see Table 39).

Table 39

Would Move If Given the Opportunity n = 218

	f	%
No	142	65.1
Yes	68	31.2
No response	8	3.7

Those who responded that they would consider moving qualified their responses in terms of desired characteristics of another locale. To a considerable extent these open-ended responses clustered around the "relational" and "rootedness" responses as indicated in Table 37. The desire for materially improved housing was not expressed. At the same time Keller's (1968) findings, also Carp (1976) need to be considered. The responses could have been influenced by the lack of viable housing alternatives for themselves. At the point of conducting the study no plans for construction of new low-income housing for Latino elderly could be found in the study area's public or private sector so as to effectively guage the interviewers' responses to possible options. In effect, such options were nonexistent for the study group.

Group and leisure activities.

Within the study population 56 percent (122 respondents) reported membership in an organized group. The remaining 96 (44 percent) reported no such memberships. Within 122 reporting group membership, 61 (50.8 percent) indicated they belonged to recreational groups, while 35 (28.7 percent) showed religious group membership. The remaining 25 (20.5 percent) indicated participation in a variety of social clubs (see Table 40).

Table 40

Type of Group Membership $n = 122$

Group	f		%	
Recreational	62		50.8	
Religious	35		28.7	
Work-related	4		3.3	
Political	4		3.3	
Nutritional	1	25	0.8	20.5
Other (mixed auspices, e.g., senior citizens' center)	16		13.1	

When asked in more detail about the nature of their leisure activities and whether they engaged in them alone, with family, friends, or an organized group, two-thirds of the study group, 145 respondents (66.5 percent), reported that they primarily engaged in leisure time activity alone. (See Table 41.)

Table 41

Type of Involvement in Leisure Activities $n = 218$

Type	f	%
Alone	145	66.5
With family	38	17.4
With friends	15	6.9
With organized group	20*	9.2

* NOTE: The 20 respondents reporting group involvement in their leisure time activities were all members of some type of group and represent 16.4 percent of the total Latino subgroup who reported group membership, $n = 122$.

The more general social environment.

Since the interview guide provided an extended conversational format, the respondents were encouraged to talk on any number of themes including current social conditions. These open-ended discussions involved a host of topics which ranged from respondent opinions on child rearing procedures to their perspectives on moral issues. In the course of this process, the interviewees were asked to sum up how present conditions compared with what they had known earlier in their adult lives. In response, 119 (54.6 percent) indicated the view that life circumstances today were worse, while 76 (34.9 percent) stated that in their opinion things were better (see Table 42).

Immediately observable to the interviewers, however, were a host of qualifying statements surrounding either the positive or negative responses recorded in the interview guide. The 76 interviewees who gave positive responses invariably stated that they were speaking only about their material circumstances. The Social Security benefits were described as an improvement over their previous financial conditions. At the same time, those 76 respondents indicated that they thought the weakening of traditional family values and the lack of respect for the elderly were creating worse circumstances than those they knew in their youth. In a like manner, those 119 who indicated that conditions were worse now, clarified that they meant with regard to moral familial and mutualistic values; the same 119 reported that they themselves were in better circumstances with regard to their financial or material circumstances.

Table 42
Social Conditions $n = 218$

See conditions as	f	%
Better	76	34.9
Worse	119	54.6
About the same	8	3.6
No response	15	6.9

Concept of Aging

The respondents were questioned as to what constituted old age. Approximately one-quarter of the interviewees indicated chronological age as the criterion—53 respondents (24.3 percent). At the same time the open-ended responses to this question indicated considerable variance as to the appropriate age, which ranged anywhere from 55 to 72 years old. Beyond this, the response pattern emerged as a wide range of mixed considerations leaning toward either physical or mental status (see Table 43).

Table 43
What Determines When a Person Is Old $n = 218$

Factors	f		%	
Chronological Designation				
Age	53		24.3	
Physical States				
Appearance	6		2.8	
Can't Work	9		4.2	
Mental States				
State of Mind	33 ⎫		15.1 ⎫	
Dependent	43 ⎬		19.7 ⎬	
Mixed Mental/Physical States	⎪	143	⎪	65.5
Both together	57 ⎬		26.1 ⎬	
Other to include physical	10 ⎭		4.6 ⎭	
No response	7		3.2	

If a type of response pattern emerged within the Latino elders group it was that mental states were seen as interwoven to some extent in the definition of aging by approximately two-thirds, 65.5 (65 percent), of the respondents. But again, the responses lacked enough clarity to arrive at a more positive determination.

VI. ANALYSIS OF FINDINGS AND CONCLUSIONS

A Study Group for Future Comparative Study

A summary profile of the 218 respondents who comprised the San Diego Latino elders study group indicates the following characteristics:

- Their average age was 68.1 years. They ranged in age from 52 to 95.
- Their average income was $345 per month.
- Only 7.3 percent were on welfare and only 1.8 percent were dependent upon family for sustenance. The remainder of the study group were on employment-related income programs such as pensions, with 60 percent receiving Social Security, 13 percent still employed, and 45 percent homeowners.
- The group averaged 5.8 years of formal education, although 23.1 percent had never attended formal school.

If the profile could be further summarized in characteristics of significance to the study, these would include the following: first, the inquiry tapped into a residentially stable population with 56.5 percent having lived in their present residence six years or more, while only 9.1 percent had been living less than one year in their present residence. This factor allowed the study access to "established residents" rather than newcomer interactional patterns. Second, the study interviewed Latinos who had relatively long exposure to the United States cultural ambience. A total of 52 (23.9 percent) had been born in the continental United States. Of the remaining 166 respondents there was no clear data for 10, yet 150 (96.1 percent) had resided on the mainland eleven years or more. This permitted the inquiry the opportunity to search out and examine what Edmonson (1958:1) terms institutional values—in this instance Latino cultural patterns—in the context of the pressures of the Anglo majority cultural ambience.

The inclusion of 50-year-olds in the study group did in fact have some verification at the end of the project. A check of community-based agencies serving Latino elders confirmed the community consultants' observations prior to initiating the study that some persons younger than 55 do participate with older Latinos in agency programs for the elderly. Subsequent observations made by the researcher group indicate that some 50-year-olds may well be the natural peers of the older Latinos. The exact percentage of such younger participants in aging programs in San Diego could not be determined. At the same time, the small number included in the study, namely 8 respondents (3.6 percent of the total study group) who ranged in age from 52 to 54, would appear to reflect the actual situation.

Impact and significance.

While the research intent has not been to generalize the San Diego study population information to the total population of Latino elders nationwide, the information developed is seen as having a useful research function. The demographic parameters, the value dimensions and the interactional patterns of the San Diego Latino study group can serve as baseline data for comparative study among other Latino elderly groups.

Indicators of Ethnicity

Two indicators of Latino ethnicity for possible use if future research emerged from the study. The first centered on self-identifying terms used by the respondents, as well as the manner in which these terms emerged within the context of the interview. The second centered on the language preferences of the study group.

It was clear that the respondent group overwhelmingly identified themselves in terms of point of national origin or cultural heritage. Of the total sample, 80.2 percent identified themselves as *Mexicanos* (Mexicans). This included respondents of Mexican heritage who had been born in the United States. Another 10.1 percent identified as *Puerto Riqueños* regardless of length of residence on the mainland. Still another 1.8 percent identified according to specific Latin American countries of origin. Only a miniscule 4.6 percent identified as *Mexican American*.

In reviewing the interview process, the ethnic identification could come anywhere in the interview but occurred most frequently during those interview items related to questions and issues where the respondent was asked to recollect his or her earlier life. The item of importance linked to this feature of the research was the fact that in three-quarters of the situations, the self-identifier emerged naturally in an unsolicited fashion within the *plática* interview.

The second ethnic indicator which emerged from the research was the overwhelming preference for Spanish by the study group. Explicit preference for Spanish was indicated by 83.9 percent of the study group. In actual fact, 95.4 percent of the interviews were conducted in that language. As will be recalled, the methodology had permitted the respondents to gravitate to their language of preference during the interview whether or not a language preference had been stated explicitly.

Significance.

Those findings would appear to have relevance for outside individuals and/or organizations interfacing with the study population. First, researchers and providers would find that these Latino elders are firm as to their own ethnic identification. Moreover, researchers would find that if the respondents are given the opportunity, they will provide their own self-labeling within the context of the interview situation. It may well be that the problem of ethnic designation for Latino populations which plagues census-type studies is soluble. Latino elderly populations need not be force-fitted into the confines of non-applicable labels. Second, Latino elders would appear to prefer Spanish as the language of interaction. Moreover, if provided the opportunity, the Latino elders as a group would appear also to indicate their preference for Spanish in higher ratios than as reported in census data. The 1970 census information indicates that 71.9 percent of the 55-64 age group stated their preference for Spanish. For the 65-plus age group, the preference was higher, namely 85.4 percent. It should be noted that perhaps these and other like estimates might be below the actual natural flow of language preference among Latino elders.

On the basis of the San Diego experience, the researchers would venture that similar patterns for ethnic self-identification and Spanish language preference may well prevail for other populations of Latino elderly having a similar profile. Obviously this requires validation through further study.

The Primary Networks

The respondents reported relatively active interaction patterns with kinship networks. Of the total study, 88.3 percent had family in their immediate vicinity or neighborhood, 83.3 percent reported kin outside of the San Diego area and 6.6 percent were in at least weekly contact with these networks. By their self report, 57.5 percent of the respondents indicated that they were pleased with the present frequency of contact (see Table 28), while 42 percent indicated desiring more contact.

The activity of the primary networks was also evident as to whom the respondents would turn at the point of a crisis. Here, there was evidence of the inclusion of non-kin, namely friends and neighbors, in the networks. At the point of immediate need, 70.2 percent of the respondents indicated they would first turn to family and an additional 12.8 percent indicated they would turn to friends and neighbors.

The quality of their neighborhoods also emerged as a possible factor for consideration in the respondents' primary networks. A major portion of the study group, 89 percent of the Latino elders, expressed some form of satisfaction and/ or approval of their present neighborhoods, and when asked if they would move for any reason, slightly over two-thirds (65.1 percent) had no comment with regard to any reasons for desiring to move.

It also appeared that the respondents themselves functioned in primary network links, assisting either elders of Latinos in general. Within the research, 11.5 percent were found to be engaged in a wide range of helping activity on a more communitywide basis within what has been identified as the servidor system.

At the same time, several key respondent attitudes toward their primary networks emerged in the context of the total interview. The respondents indicated they would first turn to family and friends in crisis. They also indicated openness to accepting outreach assistance from these networks, including the study's own interviewers. As it developed, 63.8 percent accepted linking services from the interviewers. In almost the same breath, though, the respondents indicated a strong sense of self-reliance, of not wanting to impose, and of even not expecting assistance from family and friends as their right. This quality was noted as a feeling of *orgullo* (pride) in avoiding any dependency on others. It is notable that even among those 20 respondents who were living as dependents with their family, half expressed the desire to live independently. Finally, when asked who had responsibility for overall problems resolution, almost three-quarters (73.4 percent) of the interviewees indicated the government *(el gobierno)*. None mentioned the primary networks of either family or friends as a final recourse.

Significance.

Outside individuals and organizations planning to interface with the study group would find the reliance on and use of primary networks by the Latino elders to be more complex than might first appear on the surface. The elders value close proximity to as well as interaction with their primary networks. At the same time, Latino elders would appear also to value highly their independence from these networks. Moreover, they do not look to the networks for major problem resolution. They would appear to utilize these networks as linkage steps to get to those agencies and resources which can serve their needs. In the instance of the San Diego study population, the respondents' primary network would appear to play a supportive, rather than an overall provider, role in assisting the respondents in emotional coping and in meeting needs. The researchers would predict that further study will reveal similar basic patterns among other Latino elderly populations.

Emergent Needs and Apparent Contradictions

As the research progressed, matched sets of opposite opinions and at times open contradictions emerged from the Latino respondent group. These contrasts were expressed in a variety of areas beyond those cited immediately above.

As reported, 60 percent of the 218 Latino respondents had been patients in a health facility since reaching status of elders. As an initial response, though, the interviewees did not particularly express health needs as an area of greatest concern. Only 35.8 percent of the interviewees mentioned health as a priority concern. Moreover, in the open-ended context of the interview, it appeared that whenever ill health or some incapacity was mentioned, the respondents would quickly express the notion that such was to be endured, or that one had to be grateful for whatever health one had at the moment, or that others of their acquaintance were in poorer health than themselves.

The same pattern of contrasts was evident with regard to transportation. When asked if transportation was available to them, 84.8 percent responded that it was, but then qualified their answer. They reported that they did have transportation for crises, but not for their immediate and day-to-day concerns, such as shopping or for conducting personal business such as banking, or for socializing and recreation purposes. This contrast in responses was further highlighted by the call for more transportation services by almost half (44.5 percent) of the study.

An equally interesting series of contrasts has already been cited with regard to using their primary networks. As reported, the respondents turned overwhelmingly to their primary networks for immediate difficulties or at the point of crisis. At the same time, it is important to report that the respondents often expressed a qualifying reluctance to turn to anyone for help. As one respondent stated, *"bueno si iria a mi hija, pero nada mas si no hubiece remidio"* (Yes, I would turn to my daughter, but only if there were no other alternatives).

Another interviewee responding to the same issue said, *si le pido ayuda si no puedo yo sola"* (Yes, I can ask for help if I can't meet my own needs alone).

A similar set of contrasting impressions emerged with regard to the respondents' views of the formal human services and the actual patterns of interaction with these systems. On the surface, it might appear that the interviewees had little contact with and perhaps not much knowledge about the use of services. Subsequent probing during the interview, as well as observations made by the interviewers, revealed that indeed the interviewees were familiar with and utilized some human services. Moreover, despite their self-dependent attitudes, the interviewees did accept linking assistance to services.

In a similar manner, the respondents were noncommittal with regard to their expectations of treatment from the human services, as well as what they expected from agency personnel. Approximately three-quarters of the respondents could offer no recommendations as to the quality of services. Yet, as reported in Table 34, the interviewees were quite vocal in their expectations of how the elderly should be treated. This included graphic discussions around such concepts as *respeto* (respect) and *dignidad* (dignity).

These same patterns of contrasts were evident in still other areas of the interview. For example, well over half (56 percent) of the respondents reported membership in some organized group or association. At the same time when it came to their leisure activity, an overwhelming two-thirds (66.5 percent) indicated that they preferred such leisure activities on their own, rather than in groups (see Table 41).

This pattern held also with regard to the more open-ended life satisfaction aspects of the research wherein the respondents were asked whether life for them now was better or worse. Regardless of whether respondents answered positively or negatively, they immediately qualified their answers. In the main, it depended more on where the respondent started the response. If they began their response around their economic circumstances, they would state that their circumstances were better now than at earlier points in their lives. If the respondents began with a discussion of current values, moral conditions and family life, they could be counted on to describe a worsening picture.

In the course of the research the interviewers noted a distinct pattern among the respondents. First, despite the level of plática intimacy attained, the interviewees on all counts appeared reticent to spell out a list of their own needs. Second, there appeared to be an expectation on the part of the respondent that the interviewer would be sensitive enough to spot major needs. Once these had been so identified, the respondent would then engage in a lengthy description of his or her major problems, whether this were health, transportation, economic or some combination thereof.

Impact and significance.

First, individuals and organizations working with the Latino study group would need to realize that the initial response may not be the complete response. The Latino elder may not comment directly on a question or issue and may rather expect the interviewer to locate the difficulty or problem. In other instances the respondent may well couch the statement of need or difficulty in terms of referring to others with seeming greater need. Second, cultural sensitivity is needed on the part of the interviewers to assist in sorting through such dichotomies and to identify them as part of such Latino group features as previously discussed under the concept of *orgullo* (pride and self-reliance). Third, persons working with the study group would have to recognize that the emergent contradictions are more apparent than actual. They would, therefore, need to use an information-gathering approach which allows apparently contradictory responses and observations to be assessed contextually side-by-side.

From an overall perspective, researchers may find that Latino elders in general will react negatively to being confronted directly as to their needs. This was the case in San Diego. The researchers would suggest this as a fruitful area for further research and an area having considerable importance in plotting out the Latino elders' critical path to services.

Helping and Being Helped

As has been previously stated, two-thirds of the respondents, 149 (68.3 percent), were found in a helping mode themselves. Their help extended to varying forms as well as levels of activity. The greater portion, 110 (73.8 percent) of the helping subgroup, provided local neighborhood-type assistance. This included such small favors as helping with ingredients for meals or at times even providing temporary housing for other elders in need. The persons operating in this mode were termed *los vecinos* (the local neighborhood link persons and service brokers). Another small subgroup numbering 14 (9.4 percent) were not actually able to engage in helping activity at the point of the inquiry due to their present incapacity which was primarily health related. From the context of the interview, though, it could be determined that these persons had been active as helpers earlier in their lives. They were classed as "potential natural helpers". A core group of 25 individuals (16.8 percent of the helping subgroup, n = 149 or actually 11.5 percent of the total study population) were found to be providing supportive and linking services on a communitywide basis. Those persons were termed the *servidores comunicativos*. The complete natural helping network encountered has been termed the *servidor* system within the present research. The critical feature of this natural helping system is that it is seen as existing and operating parallel to the human services agencies. Moreover, there is every indication that the system as a whole is positively disposed to the human services and actively assists individuals, specifically Latino elders, to link up to services.

Despite the reluctances noted to admit need directly, it was clear that the respondents did accept being helped. As also described, they accepted services from the interviewers themselves. As it developed, these services were primarily informational and referral, transportation, translation and advocacy type in nature. It is important to indicate, though, that agency persons and professionals did not feature extensively as an initial helping resource. Only 6 percent of the study group indicated that they first turned to such persons for assistance. The exception was in health areas where 20.6 percent of the respondents reported turning to professionals first for assistance in terms of major illness. Moreover, as also previously reported, approximately three-quarters (73.4 percent) of the respondent group appeared receptive to governmental intervention as a solution to overall needs or difficulties. Lastly, while the population did appear to lack accurate information as to a number of areas of the human services, the barrier appeared to be one of knowledge rather than one of refusal to engage these systems.

Significance.

It can be expected that persons and/or organizations interfacing with the study population would find a natural helping resource in the servidor system. Moreover, these same persons and/or organizations would find the study population receptive to being helped, although this latter might not be immediately apparent. Here the capability to assess apparently contradictory information emerges again along with the importance of the style used for extending assistance. In the San Diego group there was some lack of knowledge and misinformation about the formal human service networks, but hostility toward services was nowhere encountered in the respondent group. Evidence of culturally-based antipathy toward service utilization likewise did not register within the study. The researchers would suggest that this same configuration may well hold true for other Latino elderly populations although this as other study findings now await validation through further study.

A Natural Helping Network: The Servidor System in Detail

Having located the different levels of natural helpers within the study population, the interviewers were able to more closely observe their activities. First, it must be made clear that the 149 respondents identified as in a helping mode were not all necessarily in helping interaction with each other. Moreover, their helping activity extended beyond assisting elders only. The helpers were noted as extending their help to members or other ethnic groups, although Latinos were seen as the principal beneficiaries of the servidores' attention. Second, the system as outlined below in Figure 4, must be understood to be more fluid in nature with many situational variations as to the roles of the participants.

The key actors in the natural system are seen as the servidores comunicativos (community service brokers). These individuals are readily distinguishable from other helpers within service delivery systems by the extent of their activities. Within the study the servidores comunicativos were found to be extremely versatile persons. They were most often bilingual, although several were monolingual (Spanish-speaking only). However, these latter could understand sufficient English to maintain their helping-linking activity. In addition, these persons were known by reputation by a number of individuals within their operational territory. During the course of the study the interviewers were able to note that a number of those identified as the servidores comunicativos were identified as "helping persons" by other respondents as well as by other link persons and agency personnel. The versatility of these individuals is seen as extending around a great capacity for information and referral activity along with crisis or emergency assistance. Overall, these servidores operate as catalysts and links to the utilization of services and resources.

The servidores comunicativos were also found to be quite mobile, although several did not own their own cars and depended on public transportation. One such servidora was found to be very active in Major Statistical Area 0 (Central City) and Major Statistical Area 2 (South Bay). She regularly visited five community-based senior centers, making a practice of connecting Latino elders in need with services. At times she was found to be assisting the staff of these centers to better understand their consumers' needs, acting as a translator buffer between both. This same individual was found to have a very workable knowledge of the agency networks in the two areas of San Diego in which she was active. Moreover, she knew the key agency personnel in a number of agencies who were well disposed or receptive to working with the Latino elderly.

In the North County portion of the study area (Major Statistical Area 4) several very active servidores comunicativos were found. At the time the study was conducted a number of these persons were still active on committees and in supportive service delivery throughout the area. Further inquiry indicated that some of these servidores had been instrumental in helping to initiate services and programs for the seniors in the North County area. Moreover, wherever programs serving Latino seniors were located in the study, servidores were encountered actively at work in the background.

Two other levels of servidores have also been noted: la vecina (the neighbor) and el servidor de agencia (the agency link person). It should be noted that the former were identified as respondents within the study population. The latter, the agency servidores, were identified by inference in discussions with the servidores comunicativos and through the interviewers' own observations of the community processes. None of the Latino study respondents was currently found to be employed within a human service agency.

The vecina (female) or vecino (male), the neighbor-type of servidor, was found to be a vital link in the natural helping network. This was often the individual who located the person in need or to whom the person in need would come for assistance at the neighborhood level. Usually the vecina was not found to be much more knowledgeable about services than the ordinary population, but she did know the servidores comunicativos or often did have some agency contact to whom the person in need could be referred.

The agency link persons were still another level of the helping system. The interviewers noted that the comunicativos often already had scouted out the existing agencies or services in their operating territory and had often located such key individuals within agencies who were disposed to extending services to Latinos in culturally appropriate modes. These servidores de agencia in most instances were Latino staff members of human service agencies. In a number of instances they were not. One such individual was an Anglo staff member of the Welfare Department serving the Central City-Logan Avenue area. This individual, although at first not bilingual, made every effort to receive the Latinos, young and old, with the expected courtesies as described in Table 33. While never totally fluent in Spanish this individual did acquire enough of the language to use appropriate forms of address particularly with the Latino elders. The agency servidor is a key to the observed natural helping system in that he or she, regardless of rank within the agency, provides access to services in a style acceptable to the Latino consumer. Unfortunately the inquiry could not focus on the agency servidor beyond the indirect observations of several such individuals active with respondents within the limits of the study communities. In some instances but not all, it appeared that the servidores de agencia were the servidores comunicativos themselves who had been hired by the agencies at a paraprofessional level. However, professionals with university degrees could also be found among these servidores.

Figure 4 summarizes the natural helping network or the servidor system as encountered. As noted previously, the key link persons were the servidores comunicativos who were in touch with all of the levels of helpers as well as the persons in need.

Figure 4

The Servidor System: A Natural Latino Helping Network

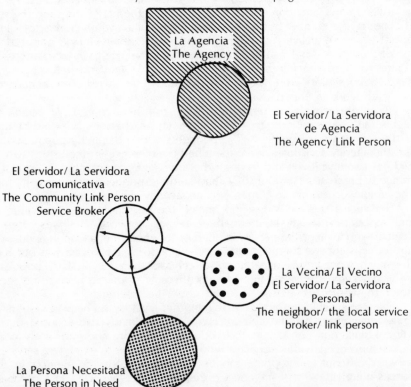

The activity of the systems as reported by the interviewers was one of linkage and supportive service provision. The servidores comunicativos and the vecinos in particular, were not able actually to meet the needs themselves: for example, providing jobs or long-term health care, or a base-line income for the Latino in need. Rather, the servidores' function was described as one of getting the potential Latino consumer whenever possible to the service corresponding to the need (or needs) encountered. Within this arrangement even the agency servidor served as a conduit or link person by mobilizing the resources of his or her respective agency in the attempt to meet the needs of the Latino applicant.

The literature reviewed in the course of the study provides supportive confirmation of the presence of natural helping networks among Latino populations. Kent (1971) has identified a system of natural helpers in Colorado which he termed *consejeras* (community counselors). These *consejeras* are described as indigenous Latino helpers functioning between different levels of government and their respective home communities. Valle (1974) describes a similar phenomenon located in Houston and San Antonio, Texas termed *conjuntadores*.

Impact and significance.

Persons seeking to interface with the Latino study population will find an extensive supportive network to assist them in making and maintaining contact. The system will be found to have varied actors and operational styles and most likely will already be in some form of interaction with the agency or professional seeking to contact the Latino elder. Verification of such networks is expected through further inquiry.

Critical Path to Services

Given the preceeding findings, the data provide a notion of the Latino respondents' critical path to the networks of the human services. With regard to the study population the pathway to the human services can be described through the complex interplay of respondent attitudes and actions. These are summarized in Figure 5.

First, it appears that a number of normative and value considerations intervene at the point where the Latino elder will act to meet his or her needs. The exact understanding of the complex interplay of the attitudes encountered, though, could not be fully explored within the present research. With regard to the San Diego findings, however, the contradictions encountered in respondent attitudes are more apparent than actual. They do not serve as permanent barriers to services. It would appear that the style and approach of the intervening persons have considerable bearing on the ability of the Latino elder to work through these attitudinal postures. The building of confianza (trust) and the maintaining of amistad (mutuality) appear to be key intervener elements. Second, in proceeding a step further to meet his or her needs, it appears that the Latino elder will seek out primary network intervention before going ahead to the human service agency. This network intervention will be of two sorts. The Latino elder will reach out to the natural networks or the natural networks will engage in outreach activity to the elder. The former pattern was quite apparent in that respondents reported that at the point of crisis or need 83 percent of the study group sought out the networks. This included 70.2 percent who sought out family and 12.8 percent who turned to friends and neighbors. The latter pattern was evident in the functioning of the servidor system as already described.

It is significant that only 6 percent of the study group proceeded directly to the human services. In addition, another 9.6 percent reported not arriving at any service at all, indicating they might withdraw to themselves with needs unmet. Whether this group remains in the posture indefinitely is uncertain. The present study also cannot offer explanations as to the actual reasons why this latter behavior occurs. Both questions are suggested as areas for further study.

Figure 5
The Latino Elder: Critical Path to Services

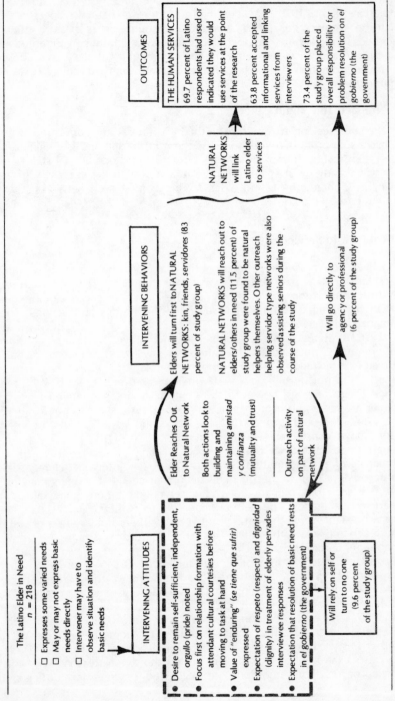

/ R. Valle & L. Mendoza |

NOTE: Percentages based on data in Tables 7, 28, 29, 31, and 35.

Impact and significance.

Persons interfacing with groups similar to the study population will find the population receptive to service utilization if attention is first paid to the respondents' attitudinal and value states. Such persons will also find receptivity if there is recognition that the respondents will not likely turn first to their primary networks rather than to the formal services at the point of crisis. These postures do not indicate cultural antipathy toward services. Respondents do go to services and look outside of their primary networks for ultimate problem resolution.

Persons interfacing with groups similar to the study population will most likely also find that their interactions will have to be "brokered." In this regard service providers and researchers interfacing with the Latino study groups can expect to find brokerage resources already in place in the Latino elders' primary networks, and in the servidor system as outlined. Moreover, they can expect to find servidores (natural helpers) to assist in the brokering process among the potential client of respondent populations. As with the other San Diego study findings the researchers hold the expectation that further research will verify such patterns.

Limitations of the Inquiry

The research missed a number of relatively easy opportunities to obtain key information. For example, with a minimum of effort the amount of property taxes paid by those who had fully amortized their homes could have been obtained. As a consequence, there was no housing cost data for almost a third of the study group, these 72 (33 percent) of the respondents were not asked the amount of their annual property taxes. Another area which was missed within the data gathering was related to present and past employment of the respondents and their spouses. The interview guide failed to specify how such information was to be obtained and recorded. As a consequence a more accurate assessment of the respondents' actual economic circumstances could not be made.

As reported above (Part V, The Methodological Limitations) two modal types of interviews emerged within the study. The shorter involved approximately three-and-one-half hours total research activity time. The longer consumed approximately four-and-one-half hours. There was no record kept of interviews that were spread over two or more days. A simple time accounting form for enumerating the exact hours employed, as well as the fractions thereof, would have provided explicit information from which to quantify interview time. As a consequence, the interview length reported is at best a generalized estimate. This data loss is all the more important in that a close reading of the shorter and longer interviews does not indicate major differences in the quality of the interview data or the level of plática attained. It appears that idiosyncratic elements determined interview length and not the substance of the information being obtained. A precise delineation of the shorter interview would then have provided a clear indicator of time investment factors for future implementation of the plática interview strategy.

The interview instrument encountered some limitations. The interview guide to an extent suffered in its Spanish language version. For example the Spanish terms for services (servicios) and for agency (agencia) appeared unclear to any number of respondents (see Appendix B). Some of the human service terminology in English appeared to lose its meaning when translated to Spanish and in fact seemed to have no direct colloquial-Spanish counterparts. This factor could help account for the high number of nonapplicable responses with regard to interviewee opinion as to the capabilities needed by agency personnel in providing services (see Tables 24 and 25). The suspicion that the instrument may have been at fault was borne out by the fact that elsewhere in the research the respondents were not at all reticent to voice their views on the qualities expected from persons interacting with the elderly (see Table 34). By the time the difficulty was pin-pointed the research was already well underway and could not be totally corrected.

The research focus also served as a limitation. The overall impetus of the inquiry was in documenting lifestyles, value outlooks and coping patterns primarily from the perspective of the Latino elder. This precluded exploration of the type of services best suited to their needs or the actual extent of knowledge of Latino elders by agency personnel in the human service delivery systems of the study area. These and other like research concerns await further study.

Finally, as stated throughout the inquiry, the San Diego study was a pilot inquiry. Both the methodology and the population findings now await validation through future study. In a sense rather than serving only as a limitation, this factor is seen as providing an informational base and a tested vehicle for additional research among Latino and minority elderly, and perhaps even the elderly in general.

Two Principal Conclusions

Two overall conclusions emerge within the study as a whole. First, the researchers were impressed with the importance of contextual analysis. It was critical to the study both to record and analyze information in terms of the situational conditions in which the information was obtained. In this manner the investigators were able to incorporate the observed behaviors with direct statements as encountered. From the researchers' standpoint, Sieber's (1973) predictions about the complementary features of combining unobtrusive and survey research techniques into one methodology were borne out. As he indicates, "qualitative analysis" fostered by the more observational techniques brings statistical information to life. "Quantitative analysis" in turn guards against the simple recording of anecdotal information. Contextual analysis is seen as particularly applicable to the Latino elderly respondent. It allows research communication to proceed in ways which are close to the ordinary patterns of interactions of the elder within his or her social environment. The researchers are of the opinion that if attention had not been paid to the methodological features comprising the plática methodology, the data obtained would not only have been skewed, but would also have emerged as less intelligible.

Second, the researchers were struck with the varities of natural network resources among the Latino populations studied. In actual fact these resources were incorporated into the study as interviewers. Upon entering the project these persons brought a natural expertise which greatly aided in implementing the research strategy. As the study progressed it was clear that these individuals were also the type of personnel who came to be identified as servidores (service link brokers) to other individuals.

VII. Implications

As has been noted extensively throughout this report, the study of Latino elders, as well as the study as a whole, was undertaken as a pilot inquiry. It proceeded along the lines of an alternative field research methodology. The implications of the study are therefore presented with the understanding that they are directly applicable to the San Diego population studied. At the same time the findings provide a series of open considerations for gerontologists seeking to interface with Latino populations.

Overall Implications

From an overall perspective it would appear that language and style go hand-in-hand when one approaches the Latino elder. It is not enough just to be proficient in the Spanish language. There are also culturally expected modes of interaction, some of which include the following: (1) an awareness of the respondents' desire to be treated with respeto and dignidad; (2) an awareness that the Latino elder has a strong desire for independence expressed variously and partially encompassed within the concept of orgullo; (3) recognition that the researchers' attention must first focus on the interactional features of the intended relationship while remaining alert to the proper cues for moving ahead within the interview itself.

With regard to the interactional expectations there is every indication that the Latino elder views the research situation as an "incipient interpersonal relationship" as described by Stebbins (1971). There is evidence that the Latino elder, as well as his or her supportive networks, seek first to test out the potentials for a relationship with a stranger or outsider regardless of whether that person is identifiable as a member of the same ethnic group. The platica methodology and its cultural augmentation features were designed to flow with this feature. Basically this approach allows the potential client, participant and/or respondent to engage in the process at his or her own pace. The present inquiry was not equipped to explore the cultural basis for this and other similar behaviors, but presents the data as material for further inquiry.

This would imply that it is not enough to approach the Latino elder strictly from a bilingual stance. There is a parallel expectation of bicultural expertise on the part of the interviewer. Both are necessary to build a culturally syntonic (culturally appropriate and harmonious) approach. The methodology as described herein is seen as meeting this dual expectation. However complex it might appear in its present narration, there is every indication that the methodology did approximate what the literature discusses as the "natural flow" of respondent interaction as well as of community events. In this context the interviewers' linguistic and cultural expertise merged into culturally syntonic research behaviors.

From an overall perspective it would seem that the methodology contains several efficiencies over the long run, despite its initial time-intensive features. In using the methodology researchers can expect the following outcomes: First, the researchers can attain a standing presence in the social environment which endures over time. Second, the researchers will find that specific interview experiences generate the possibility of other types of future interventions, including service provision. Moreover, such enduring relationships can serve in maintaining communicational and community participation ties with Latino elderly groups and the Latino community in general. Third, the research approach would appear to have considerable utility in uncovering the natural human resources such as the servidor system.

Taken collectively these efficiencies contain possible long range importance for policy makers and service providers, as well as for researchers. For example, through adaptation of the methodology, decision makers and providers can have ready access to the natural resources available in the community within specific ethnic groups. Such access might well have impact for cutting into the rising costs of care for the elderly. An added feature is that additional products might well become available from single interventions. For example not only would resources be uncovered but more permanent community relations would also be established.

As a regular expectation researchers, providers and planners can expect to find supportive natural networks among the Latino elderly. These networks will be found providing varying types of support and will be put to a wide range of uses by the Latino elders themselves. Providers, for example, can expect to find such networks within their own client or consumer populations.

These same researchers, providers and planners can expect also to find considerable differentiation in the roles and activities of the principal actors of these natural networks. For example these networks can be expected to include small numbers of highly effective natural helpers whose activities will approximate those individuals termed servidores comunicativos within the present study. In addition to these persons human service agencies may well have possibly unrecognized and far underutilized resources in terms of the agencies' own servidores de agencia (agency link persons). These are persons who may or may not be Latinos themselves but who presently avail themselves of bicultural as well as bilingual techniques in interfacing with Latino individuals and groups. These servidores de agencia along with the servidores comunicativos may be more active than previously ascertained in bringing resources to bear on the needs of the Latino elderly.

At the same time providers, planners and researchers should be aware that these natural systems are seen as supportive only by the Latino users. There is evidence that these systems are used primarily as a linking step in the process of meeting basic needs. They are not seen as the ultimate resource for problem resolution. Rather, the evidence goes in the opposite direction. The Latino elder views the solution to basic problems as resting outside his or her primary system. However generalized the notion, the San Diego study respondents placed the responsibility on el gobierno (the government).

In terms of obtaining information from the Latino elder respondent (and/or consumer), it is important to note that the initial interview response may not be the only response nor even the complete answer to a specific question or issue.

The provider, planner and/or researcher needs to maintain a contextual approach in which not only the verbal but also nonverbal and observational data are incorporated into any analysis of the information reviewed. The failure to do so may well explain why there is so much current confusion in gerontological circles about Latino elderly vis-a-vis their relationships with the human services. In one study one reads that Latino elders will not use services. Another study maintains the contrary view. The same confusion occurs in conferences and planning meetings. What may be occurring, however, is the reporting of incomplete data. By way of example within the present inquiry, it might at first glance appear that the Latino elders hardly used or knew about services, but a second look uncovered that they did use them. Not only that, but they responded positively to outreach efforts aimed at linking them to services.

In this same vein, providers, planners and researchers may need to keep in mind that contradictions in information provided by the respondent may be apparent contradictions only. In actual fact these contradictions reflect the complex interplay of intervening factors involved in the Latino elders' critical path to the human services. What remains unclear in the present research is the full exploration of such intervening factors, along with an understanding of the relative weights of various factors in determining the actions of individual Latino elders. These now await future inquiry. All in all it does not appear that the Latino elder has a built-in hostility to the human services or their utilization. Rather, the reverse is true: the elders do desire to have their needs met, but have different ways for both voicing need and for accepting help. If there is any barrier, it may rest with the provider systems which may lack understanding of the Latino elders. It may also rest in a lack of knowledge of how to use culturally compatible outreach and natural supportive systems.

Persons interfacing with the Latino elder can expect a clear-cut sense of ethnic self-identifcation. In this context the problems of labeling may rest more with outside systems and their attendant methodologies than with Latino consumers and/or respondents. Labeling problems can be removed by initiating interview procedures which allow such identification in the context of the interaction. Ethnic self-identification can be expected to vary from individual to individual. In addition, local and regional variations are to be expected. At the same time, for that cohort of Latinos age 50 or more years, the self-identification most likely will rest with the individual's place of national and/or cultural origin.

As an added feature, providers, planners and researchers can expect to find a wide range of value and attitudinal clues to accompany the respondents' use of ethnic self-identifiers. Most of these will center around a strong and healthy sense of identity. The San Diego interviewers noted very strong, positive feelings surrounding the total area of ethnic self-identification. Moreover, the respondents' self-identifier usually brought with it a host of associated cultural values. Persons interfacing with the Latino elder group may well find this area to be very sensitive but yet very rich in providing information if properly approached within the methodology used. Among the San Diego respondents the statements *soy Mexicano* or *soy Puerto Riqueño* carried considerable verbal and nonverbal impact at the point of declaration.

Along with a strong sense of self-identification outside individuals may well find that there is also acceptance of some generic designations by Latino elders. These designations may well vary from region to region. The term Latino as used throughout this report serves as a case in point. It was found acceptable in the study area although not one of the respondents used it as a self-identifier. It is incumbent on the providers, planners and/or researchers to search out those generic terms acceptable within their respective arenas.

Implications of the Plática Methodology

It is automatically understood that the present methodology awaits validation. At the same time it contains several potentially useful features even in its present form. The following suggested uses are intended to be illustrative rather than exhaustive as to potential uses.

Implications for service providers.

It would appear that with slight changes in language the plática methodology and its culturally augmented features can be made directly applicable to service providers. For example, it could be utilized for intake interviewing or for outreach interviews with potential Latino consumers. The methodology also could have application to conducting needs assessments with the community.

Implications for planners and policy makers.

The methodology as presently constituted would appear to have direct application to planners and policy makers in terms of mapping Latino elderly populations within their respective social environment as noted above. The community linkage system utilized throughout the study is seen as having specific application in initiating and maintaining active participation by Latino (and by extension other ethnic minority) constituencies in planning and policy-making processes.

Implications for researchers.

As of the termination of the study, researchers have available to them a tested and explicated methodology for replication elsewhere. The San Diego research effort also provides other investigators with a baseline profile of a Latino elder population for possible comparative analysis in other locales. As designed, the open community participation process permits the lessening of community apprehension, while at the same time providing for a variety of ongoing technical assistance products. In this regard other investigators may need to include items not regularly associated with research. For example the provision of information and referral services on request as well as an honorarium to the interviewee. The suggestion emerging from the San Diego study is that it may be considered culturally rude for researchers to take information without providing an exchange with the informant population. Finally, the methodology as outlined is amenable to "quality control" procedures corresponding to self-monitoring techniques used within both survey and unobstrusive research.

Implications of the Findings

As with the methodology, the study population findings await validation through further study. At the same time the findings on the servidor system of natural helpers suggest several immediate applications.

Implications for service providers.

Service providers may have a natural helping resource system at their fingertips which can assist them in making contact with in providing services to Latino elderly populations. Part of this resource may already exist within their own agency or program in terms of key servidores de agencia (agency link persons) who are already active and accepted by Latino consumers. This resource system as a whole can greatly facilitate the extension of the providers' presence in the social environment. It can be used as a two-way communicational system. In addition, providers will find that this system is generally supportive of, rather than competitive with, their program of services. The prime intent of the servidor system is to connect the Latino consumer with resources.

Implications for planners and policy makers.

Persons interfacing with Latino elderly populations would need to be aware that they have local resources available to them. At the same time they will need to recognize that the Latino elder will approach the initial contact stage from the standpoint of establishing relationships, rather than engaging immediately in the "planning and decision tasks." If these different perceptions remain unrecognized or are left unattended, the planners and Latino elders may find themselves with basic procedural misunderstandings. These misunderstandings could serve easily to further cloud or accelerate the normal differences which attend the interactions between planners, decision makers and ethnic minority community members..

Implications for research.

The San Diego inquiry, among a number of other studies conducted in previous years—for example, the Andrus Center Cross Cultural Studies—would serve to illustrate that natural resource persons can be combined with more technically trained personnel to produce a joint research endeavor. If invited from the beginning, servidores of varied levels will become available to the research effort and/or will facilitate its progress throughout the study area.

Closing Notes and Observations

At the initiation of the present study the researchers noted a distinct trend in the social sciences toward modification of present research paradigms. Fortunately, several key researchers in the field of gerontology have served as pioneers in such alternative undertakings. These theorists have been discussed in Part II of this report. The San Diego study saw itself as a part of this alternative collectivity.

The San Diego study would not imply that all of the major research questions regarding Latino elders have been addressed. Likewise, the study would not imply that all of the difficulties between Latino elders and service delivery systems and/or policy makers can now be automatically dispelled through the use of the plática methodology or the servidor system. Rather, researchers see that the door has been opened. A tested means is available wherein both parties can come together to meet existing needs. At its termination the present inquiry invites efforts at replication as well as validation by other researchers within the gerontological community.

GLOSSARY

Spanish word	English equivalent
Amigable	Friendly
Amistad	Mutuality and friendship
Cariño	Affection
Compartir	To share, to partake
Comprensión	Understanding
Confianza	Mutual trust and rapport
Cooperar	To cooperate
Culturally syntonic	To be in harmony, compatible with the culture
Delicadeza	Gentleness
Dignidad	Dignity, a term related to the notion of respect
La despedida	The disengagement stage of the platica interview
La entrada	The introductory stage of the platica interview
Latino	An inclusive term used to describe persons of varied Latin American heritages presently residing in the United States
Natural helper	Individuals who take the role of brokering between the residents of their particular environments and the outside systems with respect to attempting to assist them to meet their needs.
Orgullo	Pride and self-respect
Paciencia	Patience
Plática	Intimate interaction and conversation, used to describe methodology used in present study
Respeto	Respect, a term used by respondents to describe how they felt the elderly should be treated and the way they were raised to treat the elderly
Servir	To serve, assist, help
Servidor	A person who helps, a helper
Simpático	Congenial
Sociable	Sociable
Sufrir	To endure, to suffer
Vecino	Neighbor

Selected References

Area Agency on Aging of San Diego County estimated elderly population for 1975 by subregional and major statistical areas, 1975. (Formerly the Office of Senior Citizens Affairs.)

Atencio, T.   The survival of la raza despite social services. *Social Casework,* 1971, *52* (5), 262-268.

Bengston, V.L. (Ed.).   *Gerontological research and community concern: A case study of a multi-disciplinary project.* Los Angeles: Andrus Gerontology Center, University of Southern California, 1974.

Bertalanffy, L. von.   System symbol and image of man: Man's immediate socio-ecological world. In J. Gladston (Ed.) *The interface between psychiatry and anthropology.* New York: Bruner-Mazel Publishers, 1971.

Bild, B., & Havighurst, R.   *Senior citizens in great cities: The case of Chicago. Gerontologist,* 1976, Part 2, *16* (1), 4-88.

Blau, Z.S.   Changes in status and age identification. *American Sociological Review,* 1956, *21* (2), 198-202.

Blauner, R., & Wellman, D.   Toward the decolonization of social research. In J. Ladner (Ed.) *The death of white sociology.* New York: Vintage Books, 1973.

Blumer, H.   The methodological position of symbolic interactionism. *Symbolic interactionism: Perspective and method.* Englewood Cliffs, N.J.: Prentice Hall, Inc., 1969.

Boston Black United Front.   *Statement of research and on the Roxbury infant program.* Boston, May 1970. (Mimeograph.)

Campbell, D.T.   Administrative experimentation, institutional records and non-reactive measures. In J.D. Stanley (Ed.) *Improving experimental design and statistical analysis.* Chicago: Rand McNally, 1967.

Carp, F.   Some determinants of low application rate of Mexican Americans for public housing for elderly. In *U.S. Senate Special Committee on Aging. Availability and usefulness of federal programs and services for elderly Mexican Americans.* Part 4. Washington, D.C.: U.S. Government Printing Office, 1969.

―――――――――.   The living environments of older people. In R.H. Binstock and E. Shanas (Eds.) *Handbook of aging and the social sciences.* New York: Van Nostrand Reinhold and Co., 1976.

Cicourel, A.V.   *Method and measurement in sociology.* New York: The Free Press, 1968.

―――――――――.   *Cognitive sociology: Language and meaning in social interaction.* New York: The Free Press, 1974.

Clark, M.   The anthropology of aging, a new area for studies of culture and personality. *Gerontologist,* 1967, *7* (1), 55-64.

Clark, M., & Anderson, B.G.   *Culture and aging: An anthropological study of older Americans.* Springfield, Illinois: Charles C. Thomas, 1967.

Clark, M., & Kiefer, C.W.   *Social change and intergenerational relations in Japanese and Mexican American families.* Paper presented at the annual meeting of the American Sociological Association, September 1969.

Cooley, C. *Social organizations*. New York: Charles Scribner's Sons, 1909.

Counting the forgotten: The 1970 census count of persons of Spanish-speaking background in the United States. Washington, D.C.: U.S. Government Printing Office, 1974.

Cuellar, J.B. Aging and political realities. *Proceedings of the First National Conference on the Spanish Speaking Elderly*. Shawnee Mission, Kansas, 1975.

_____. On the relevance of ethnographic methods: Studying aging in an urban Mexican American community. In V. Bengston (Ed.) *Gerontological research and community concern: A case study of a multidisciplinary project*. Los Angeles: Andrus Gerontology Center, University of Southern California, December 1974.

Crouch, B. Age and institutional support: Perspectives of older Mexican Americans. *Journal of Gerontology*, 1972, *27*(4), 524-529.

Dieppa, I. Availability and usefulness of federal programs and services to elderly Mexican Americans: Problems and prospects. Part 4. U.S. Senate Special Committee on Aging. Washington, D.C.: U.S. Government Printing Office, 1969.

Edmonson, M.S. Los manitos: A study of institutional values. In M.S. Edmonson, C. Madsen, & J.F. Coller (Eds.) *Contemporary American culture*. New Orleans: Middle American Research Institute, 1968.

Freire, P. *Education for critical consciousness*. New York: Seabury Press, Continuum Books, 1973.

Garcia, E. Chicano Spanish dialects and education. *Aztlan*, 1971, *2*(1), 67-73.

Garfinkel, H. *Studies in ethnomethodology*. Englewood Cliffs, N.J.: Prentice Hall, 1967.

Garfinkel, H., & Sacks, H. On formal structures of practical actions. In J.C. McKinney & E. Tirgakian (Eds.) *Theoretical sociology perspectives and developments*. New York: Appleton-Century-Crofts, 1969.

Glaser, B.G., & Strauss, A. *The discovery of grounded theory: Strategies for qualitative research*. Chicago: Aldine Publishing Co., 1967.

Gómez, E.; Martin, H.W.; & Gibson, G. *Adaption of older Mexican Americans: Some implications for social and health programs*. San Antonio, Texas: Worden School of Social Service, Our Lady of the Lake College, 1973.

Hamilton, C. Black social scientists: Contributions and problems. In J. Ladner (Ed.) *The death of white sociology*. New York: Vintage Books, 1973.

Hernández, A., & Mendoza, J. (Eds.). *Institute on aging: An orientation for Mexican American community workers in the field of aging*. Topeka, Kansas, May 1973.

Hernández, J.; Estrada, L.; & Alvirez, D. Census data and the problem of conceptually defining the Mexican American population. *Social Science Quarterly*, 1973, *53*(4), 671-687.

Indicators of the status of the elderly in the United States. DHEW Publication No. (OHD) 74-20080. DHEW-OHD, Administration on Aging, 1971.

Kaplan, B.H. (Ed.). *Psychiatric disorder and the urban environment*. New York: Behavioral Publications, 1971.

Kaplan, O. *San Diego senior citizens needs*. San Diego, California: The Urban Observatory, 1973.

Keller, S.   *The urban neighborhood: A sociological perspective.* New York: Random House, 1971.

Kent, J.   *A descriptive approach to a community.* Boulder, Colorado: Western Interstate Commission on Higher Education, (WICHE), 1971. (A video tape lecture.)

Kiefer, C.   Notes on anthropology and the minority elderly. *Gerontologist,* 1971, 2, 94-98.

Leighton, A.   Psychiatric disorders and the social environment: An outline and a frame of reference. In B. Kaplan (Ed.) *Studying personality cross culturally.* New York: Harper & Row Publisher, 1961.

—————.   Cross-cultural psychiatry. In J. Murphy and A. Leighton (Eds.) *Approaches to cross-cultural psychiatry.* Ithaca, N.Y.: Cornell University Press, 1965.

Lewin, K. (Ed.).   *Principles of topological psychology.* New York: McGraw Hill Book Company, Inc., 1936.

Lofland, J.   *Analyzing social settings.* Belmont, California: Wadsworth Publishing Co., Inc. 1966.

Los Angeles Times. Sunday, January 9, 1977, Part 1 and 3.

Maldonado, D.   The Chicano aged. *Social Work,* 1975, *20* (3), 213-216.

Manney, J.D., Jr.   *Aging in American society.* SRS-HEW Grant No. 94-76007/501. Ann Arbor, Michigan, 1975.

Matza, D.   *Becoming deviant.* Englewood Cliffs, N.J.: Prentice Hall, 1969.

Montoya, M.   *Health services research and the Hispanic community.* Paper presented at the First Hispanic National Conference on Health and Human Services, Los Angeles, California, September 1976.

Miller, J.R.   *A critical and phenomenological analysis of the awareness by gerontologists of the function and determinative effect of value concepts in their professional activities.* Richmond: Department of Philosophy, Eastern Kentucky University, 1975. (Mimeograph.)

Moll, L.C.; Rueda, R.S.; Reza, R.; Herrera, J.; & Vásquez, L.P.   Mental health services in East Los Angeles: An urban community case study. In M. Miranda (Ed.) *Psychotherapy with the Spanish-speaking: Issues in research and service delivery.* Los Angeles: University of California at Los Angeles, 1976.

Montiel, M.   The Mexican American family: A proposed research framework. *Proceedings from the First National Conference on Spanish Speaking Elderly.* Shawnee Mission, Kansas, 1975, 38-42.

Moore, J.W.   Mexican Americans. *Gerontologist,* 1971, Part 2, *II* (1), 30-35.

—————.   Situational factors affecting minority aging. *Gerontologist,* 1971, Part 2, *II* (1), 88-93.

—————.   Social constraints on sociological knowledge: Academics and research concerning minorities. *Social Problems,* 1973, *21* (1), 65-77.

Moore, J.R., & Sánchez, D.   La plática: An approach to cultural clarification. Unpublished paper, Chicano Training Center, Fourth Annual State Institute for Chicano Social Work Education. Worden School of Social Work, San Antonio, Texas, 1976.

Murase, K.   Ethnic minority content in the social work curriculum: Social welfare policy and social research. In C.W. McCann (Ed.) *Perspectives on ethnic minority content in social work education*. Boulder, Colorado: Western Interstate Commission for Higher Education, 1972.

Murphy, J.M.   Social system concepts as cross-cultural methods for psychiatric research. In J. Murphy and A. Leighton (Eds.) *Approaches to cross-cultural psychiatry*. Ithaca, N.Y.: Cornell University Press, 1965.

Myers, V.   *Unconventional techniques for collecting survey data: A reassessment of conventional theory and practice*. Los Angeles: University of California at Los Angeles, 1974.

Neugarten, B.L.   Age groups in American society: The time of the young old. *Political consequences of aging, annals, 1974, 415,* 187-198.

Officer, J.   *Sodalities and systematic linkages the joining habits of Mexican Americans*. Unpublished doctoral dissertation, University of Arizona, 1964.

Padilla, A.; Carlos, M.L.; & Keefe, S.   Mental health service utilization by Mexican Americans. In M. Miranda (Ed.) *Psychotherapy with the Spanish speaking: Issues in research and service delivery*. Los Angeles, University of California at Los Angeles, 1976.

Peñalosa, F.   The changing Mexican American in Southern California. *Sociology and Social Research,* 1967, *51* (4), 405-417.

Persons of Spanish origin in the United States: March 1973 (advance report). *Current population reports: Population characteristics*. U.S. Dept. of Commerce, Bureau of Census, Series No. 259. Washington, D.C.: U.S. Government Printing Office, 1974.

Pfohl, S.S.   Social role analysis: The ethno-methodological critique. *Sociology and Social Research,* 1975, *59* (3), 243-263.

Proceedings of the First National Conference on the Spanish Speaking Elderly. Shawnee Mission, Kansas, 1975.

Reynoso, C., & Coppelman, P.D.   Proposals to eliminate legal barriers affecting elderly Mexican Americans. Special Committee on Aging, U.S. Senate. Washington, D.C.: U.S. Government Printing Office, 1972.

Rios, F.A.   The Mexican in fact, fiction, and folklore. *El Grito,* 1968, *II* (1), 13-26.

Rocco, R.A.   The Chicano in the social sciences: Traditional concepts, myths, and images. *Aztlan,* 1970, *I* (2), 75-97.

Romano, O.   The anthropology and sociology of the Mexican American: The distortion of Mexican American history. *El Grito,* 1968, 2 (1), 13-26.

_____   The historical and intellectual presence of Mexican Americans. *El Grito,* 1969, 2 (2), 13-26.

Schatzman, L., & Strauss, A.   *Field research: Strategies for a natural sociology*. Englewood Cliffs, N.J.: Prentice Hall Inc., 1973.

Schmidt, F.H.   *Spanish surnamed American employment in the Southwest*. Washington, D.C.: U.S. Government Printing Office, 1970.

Seward, G., & Marmor, J.   *Psychotherapy and culture conflict*. New York: The Ronald Press, 1965.

Shanas, E.   Family-kin networks and aging in cross-cultural perspective. *Journal of Marriage and the Family,* 1973, *35* (3), 505-511.

Sieber, S.   The integration of fieldwork and survey methods. *American Journal of Sociology*, 1973, *78* (6), 1335-1358.

Solis, F.   Cultural factors in programming of services for Spanish-speaking elderly. *Proceedings from the First National Conference on Spanish Speaking Elderly*. Shawnee Mission, Kansas, 1975.

Solomon, B.   Growing old in the ethno system. In E.P. Stanford (Ed.) Minority aging, proceedings of the Institute on Minority Aging. San Diego, California: Campanile Press, San Diego State University, 1974.

Sotomayor, M.   *A study of Chicano grandparents in an urban barrio*. Unpublished doctoral dissertation, University of Denver, 1973.

──────── Mexican American interaction with social systems. *Social Casework*, 1971, *52* (5), 316-324.

──────── Social change and the Spanish speaking elderly. *Proceedings from the First National Conference on Spanish Speaking Elderly*. Shawnee Mission, Kansas, 1975.

Spicer, E.H.   Persistent cultural systems: A comparative study of identity systems that can adapt to contrasting environments. *Science*, 1971, *174* (4011), 785-800.

Stebbins, R.A.   The unstructured research interview as incipient interpersonal relationship. *Sociology and Social Research*, 1972, *56* (2), 164-169.

Steglich, W.C.; Cartwright, W.; & Crouch, B.   *Study of needs and resources among aged Mexican Americans*. Lubbock: Texas Technological College, 1968.

Takagi, P.   The myth of assimilation in American life. *Amerasia Journal*, 1973, *2*, 149-158.

Torres-Gil, F.   *Los ancianos de la raza: A beginning framework for research, analysis, and policy*. Unpublished working paper, Brandeis University, Florence Heller Graduate School for Advanced Studies in Social Welfare, Waltham, Massachusetts, May 1972.

──────── *Political behavior: A study of political attitudes and political participation among older Mexican Americans*. Unpublished doctoral dissertation, Brandeis University, 1976.

──────── *The politics of los ancianos: A study of the political participation of the Chicano elderly*. Brandeis University, Waltham, Massachusetts, 1974.

Truzzi, M. (Ed.).   *Verstenen: Subjective understanding in the social sciences*. Reading, Massachusetts: Addison, Wesley Publishing Co., 1974.

U.S. Senate Special Committee on Aging.   *Availability and usefulness of federal programs and services to elderly Mexican Americans*. Parts 1-5. Washington, D.C.: U.S. Government Printing Office, 1969.

──────── *Availability and usefulness of federal programs and services to elderly Mexican Americans*. El Paso, Texas, Part II. Washington, D.C.: U.S. Government Printing Office, 1968.

U.S. Bureau of the Census.   *Population and housing: 1970 census tracts*. Final Report PHC (1)-188, San Diego, California, SMSA. Washington, D.C.: U.S. Government Printing Office, 1972.

──────── *Persons of Spanish origin in the United States, March 1971 and 1972*. Series P-20, No. 250. Washington, D.C.: U.S. Government Printing Office, 1973.

──────── *Current population reports, population characteristics: Persons of Spanish origin in the United States, March 1972*. (Advance Report) Series P-20, No. 259. Washington, D.C.: U.S. Government Printing Office, 1974.

_____ Current population reports, persons of Spanish origin in the United States, March 1975. Series P-20, No. 299. Washington, D.C.: U.S. Government Printing Office, 1976.

Vaca, N.C.   The Mexican American in the social sciences, 1912-1970. *El Grito*, 1970, *III* (3), Part I, 3-24; Part II, 1970, 4 (2), 17-51.

Valle, R.   *An analysis of compadrazgo as an indigenous webwork compared with an urban mental health network.* Unpublished doctoral dissertation, University of Southern California, 1974.

_____ Meztizo interviewer. *Mano a mano*, Chicano Training Center, Houston, Texas, 1972, *1* (2).

Villalpando, V.; Ballow, G.; Cady, J.; Pool, A.; Ramírez, M.; Torres-Stanovik, R.; & Steendam, S.   *Illegal aliens: Impact of illegal aliens on the county of San Diego.* San Diego: County of San Diego Human Resources Agency, 1977.

Webb, E.J.; Campbell, D.T.; Schwartz, R.D.; & Schrest, L.B.   *Unobtrusive measures: Nonreactive research in the social sciences.* Chicago: Rand McNally, 1966.

White House Conference on Aging: The Spanish speaking elderly, special concerns report. Washington, D.C.: U.S. Government Printing Office, 1971.

APPENDIX A: SELECTED BIBLIOGRAPHY

The following annotated bibliography is meant to be selective rather than exhaustive. The literature reviewed attempts to present a guide to the policy questions, the research issues affecting primarily the Mexican cohort of the Latino elderly group. Selected literature on natural networks and primary support systems has also been included. The problem of multiple ethnic identifiers pervaded the citations used. The researchers chose to proceed in the language of the San Diego inquiry regardless of the actual ethnic identifier used in the literature item itself. Therefore, the term Latino has been put into the discussion wherever possible. The San Diego study objectives heavily influenced both the selection of the items included as well as the issues discussed within each article. The reader is encouraged to proceed to the original article or document to get the individual author's views in full.

Bell, Duran; Kassachau, Patricia; & Zellman, Gail.   *Delivery of services to elderly members of. minority groups: A critical review of the literature.* Santa Monica, California: Rand, 1976.

Chapter three of this report addresses itself to the Latino elderly of heritage, (pp. 30-52). An extensive bibliography is included which would be of value to any researcher interested in this specific area. The review of literature on service delivery to the Latino elderly poses some questions regarding the relevancy and general validity of earlier studies. The authors fail to distinguish between social class and ethnicity variables in their analysis, though. The reader also should go to the original sources in order to obtain in-depth understanding of the issues discussed. Some problems and needs of the Latino elderly are discussed: e.g., lack of accurate census data and research studies; low income and low educational attainment, housing, health, and language problems.

Camarillo, Mateo.   Areas for research on Chicano aging. In E. Percil Stanford (Ed.) *Minority aging: Proceedings of the Institute on Minority Aging.* San Diego: The Campanile Press, San Diego State University, 1974.

The writer presents a review of studies and policies related to Latino elderly. The point that is raised is that few studies have been done of Mexican heritage. He notes there is a lack of knowledge upon which to develop adequate policies, programs and services for the Latino elderly. The writer suggests that research on Latino elderly should look at the differences and similarities of the lifestyles among Latinos of Mexican heritage, paying particular attention to culture, social structure, geographic areas and degree of urbanization.

Carp, Frances.   Housing and minority group elderly. *Gerontologist,* 1969, *9* (1), 20-24.

A study to investigate the non-utilization of low income housing by the Latino elders of Mexican heritage in San Antonio, Texas. The reasons for non-utilization were compared in terms of demographic, biographic and attitudinal variables with Anglo-American applicants to Villa Tranchese, a highrise public housing apartment house for the aged.

——————.   Communicating with elderly Mexican Americans. *Gerontologist,* 1970, *10,* 126-134.

A report of an investigation into the means by which the Latino elderly of Mexican heritage obtain information, a comparison of their communication habits and capabilities with Anglo-American elderly. The study also entertains consideration of some ways in which the community might improve communication with its older Latino members. The sample size consisted of 100 Latino elders of Mexican heritage, 62 years of age or over. One conclusion drawn was that the primary sources of information for the elderly study group were family and friends.

——————   Housing and minority group elderly. In U.S. Congress, Senate Special Committee on Aging, Part IV, Washington, D.C. Hearing, 91st Congress, First Session, January 14-15, 1969, 460-476.

Carp presents three different statements related to a study on why Latino elderly of Mexican heritage had not applied for low income housing. The study found that one determinant of non-application for public housing for the respondents was that they did not want to move and they placed great value in home ownership and interpersonal bonds with relatives and friends.

Clark, Margaret, & Kiefer, C.W.   *Special change and intergenerational relations in Japanese and Mexican American families.* Paper presented at the Annual Meeting of the American Sociological Association, September 1969.

The influence of social change upon the family was under study in a three-generational study of three ethnic subcultures in San Francisco: Anglo-American, Japanese-American, and persons of Mexican heritage. Among their findings, the authors point to the retention of ethnic group values across generations, specifically in terms of primary group interactions. The authors also cite the importance of the concept of "respect" particularly in terms of interactions with the elderly family members.

Clark, Margaret, & Mendelson, Monique.   Mexican American aged in San Francisco: A case description. *Gerontologist,* 1969, *9* (2), 90-95.

A study that investigates the specific social and cultural traits that may be germane to aging adjustments among Latino elderly of Mexican heritage. The case study of an elderly Latino respondent from the Mission District is used to illustrate the study findings on sociocultural traits of his ethnic group.

Coles, Robert.   *The old ones of New Mexico.* New York: Anchor Books, 1975.

The Latino elders who speak in Cole's book tell of their traditions and values, their language, their habits, ways of speaking to one another and religious attitudes; in short, a way of life is transmitted. A key element of work in the author's methodological style in obtaining information from the Latino elderly themselves in their natural habitat.

Crouch, Ben.   Age and institutional support: Perceptions of older Mexican Americans. *Journal of Gerontology,* 1972, *27* (4), 524-529.

The study was conducted in Lubbock, Texas. The suggestion is made by the writer that the respondents' limited use of government programs may be due to both (1) an inability to handle the bureaucratic and administrative aspects of programs and (2) language barriers. One finding of the study indicated that despite their non use of services, the Latino respondents had less overall expectation of aid from the family than from the church or government.

Cuellar, José.   On the relevance of ethnographic methods: Studying aging in an urban Mexican American community. In Vernon Bengston (Ed.) *Gerontological research and community concern: A case study of a multi-disciplinary project.* Los Angeles: Andrus Gerontology Center, University of California at Los Angeles, 1974.

The writer describes basic ethnographic techniques for the study of urbanized elderly Latinos of Mexican heritage. These techniques as applied to a research study to such persons in East Los Angeles, living in an age-segregated low-cost housing project are described.

Gómez, Ernesto; Martin, Harry W.; & Gibson, Guadalupe.   *Adaptation of older Mexican Americans: Some implication for social and health programs.* San Antonio, Texas, Worden School of Social Services, Our Lady of the Lake College, 1973. (Mimeograph.)

The researchers interviewed 200 residents of a south San Antonio barrio who were over 55 years of age. The study reports that service programs were under-utilized. The authors cite the absence of a viable information and referral system for the Latino elderly which creates linkages between them and service programs as basic to the under-utilization patterns.

Hernández, Ascención, & Mendoza, John (Eds.).   *Institute on aging: An orientation for Mexican American community workers in the field of aging.* Topeka, Kansas, May 1973.

The author reports on successful modes of training Latino community workers to provide social services to the Latino elderly. The training included (1) basic orientation to roles and functions of aging services, (2) the means to organize a statewide advocacy council, and (3) the development of strategies for attaining civil rights by the Latino elderly.

La Luz. Special feature: The Hispano aged. 1975, *4* (5), Denver, Colorado.

This issue devoted to Latino elderly has a recurrent theme throughout, for the development of culturally relevant service delivery models to service the elderly. The authors favor a search for indigenous, mutual-help systems and patterns which would be culturally relevant.

Maldonado, David.   The Chicano aged. *Social Work,* 1955, *20* (3), 213-216.

The author presents an argument against the popular sociological theory that assumes that the aged Latinos of Mexican heritage are properly cared for because of the extended family pattern. Changing patterns are reviewed and unmet social service needs are noted.

Moore, Joan.   Mexican Americans. *Gerontologist*, 1971, *2* (1), 30-35.

This article points out that there is almost no extensive research on the Latino elderly of Mexican heritage. What little there is, provides some insights but does not represent the minority point of view, not the significance of local situations with enough clarity to generalize about this population group. Moore presents a critique of gerontological studies on the Mexican American and criticizes several studies which concluded that the family remains a significant support for the Mexican American elderly. A more relevant question would be to determine how these potential resources operate or fail to operate for the Latino elderly.

National Association Pro Spanish Speaking Elderly. *Search for Hispanic models, final report.* The First Western Regional Conference on Aging. Los Angeles, California, 1976.

The objectives of this conference were (1) to identify the needs of the Latino elderly in the Western Region, and (2) to identify the processes of service delivery which take into account the cultural attributes of these elderly upon which program models could be developed. The conference proceedings highlight the issues of service delivery regarding the Latino elderly, as well as the need for bilingual, bicultural personnel. Suggestions to culturally appropriate features for services were included in the conference report.

Nuñez, Francisco.   *Variations in fulfillment of expectations of social interaction and morale among aging Mexican Americans and Anglos.* Los Angeles: University of Southern California, 1976. (Mimeograph.)

The author's review of the literature presents the principal theme of the need to maintain extended kinship networks in terms of high morale among Latino elders. At the same time, the author cites the changing nature of these networks.

Olen, Leonard.   The older rural Spanish speaking people of the Southwest. In E.G. Youmans (Ed.) *Older rural Americans.* Lexington: University of Kentucky Press, 1967.

The writer is concerned primarily with older rural Latinos. He assesses social, economic, and health status, examines their family and community roles, and presents some of their problems. The writer utilizes 1960 census data upon which to make assessments. While the analysis does provide some insight to the rural Latino elder situation, the analysis is dated.

Proceedings of the First National Conference on Spanish Speaking Elderly, 1975. Shawnee Mission, Kansas, 1975.

This conference proceeding provided a policy and research issue update on gerontological concerns from Latino elderly perspectives.

Reynoso, Cruz, & Coppelman, Peter D.   *Proposals to eliminate legal barriers affecting elderly Mexican Americans.* Working paper prepared for the Special Committee on Aging of the U.S. Senate, May 1972. Washington, D.C.: U.S. Government Printing Office, 1972.

The authors deal with the legal barriers to eligibility and full utilization of federal programs by elderly Latinos of Mexican heritage. They focus on issues of low income and health. A distinction is made between a service being available, but inaccessible because potential users do not know of its presence or how to use it. The authors indicate that services may be inaccessible because of a variety of factors, to include lack of transportation, poor health, language barriers, or the attitudes of those providing the services.

Recommendations for action, 1971 White House Conference on Aging. The Spanish speaking elderly, (Los ancianos de habla Hispana). Washington, D.C.: U.S. Government Printing Office, 1971.

The White House National Conference on Aging was expanded to include topics of special concerns of particular groups of the aged. Two conclusions drawn cite language and lack of understanding of entering human service and governmental systems as key barriers to service utilization on the part of the Latino elder. The failure of human service systems to mobilize themselves to address these issues is also cited in the report.

Sánchez, Pablo.   The Spanish heritage elderly. In E. Percil Stanford (Ed.) Minority aging: Proceedings of the Institute on Minority Aging. San Diego: The Campanile Press, San Diego State University, 1974.

The writer provides an analysis of demographic data on the Latino elderly, 65 years of age or older, based on the 1970 census.

Sotomayor, Marta.   A study of Chicano grandparents in an urban barrio. Unpublished doctoral dissertation, University of Denver, 1973.

The major intent of this study was to investigate coping patterns, cultural practices, structural arrangements and beliefs among aged grandparents. The study sample of 38 ranged in age from 55 to 91 years and resided in an urban barrio in Denver. The key familial and natural group processes and values of the respondents are explored. The issue of appropriate methodological approaches to Latino elders is explored.

_____.   The role of the aged in a colonized situation. In Ascención Hernández and John Mendoza (Eds.) Institute on aging: An orientation for Mexican American community workers in the field of aging. Topeka, Kansas: National Chicano Social Planning Council, 1973.

The writer suggests that one positive aspect of the colonization theory related to the Latino elderly of Mexican heritage has been the development and the reliance on human relationships based on kinship networks. These "natural people" arrangements of the elderly should be looked at in planning and developing services. The social injustice features of the colonization approach, though, are depreciated.

Steglich, W.C.; Cartwright, Walter; & Crouch, Ben.   Study of needs and resources among aged Mexican Americans. Lubbock: Texas Technological College, 1968.

The authors present a final report of a study conducted in Lubbock, Texas with 291 older Latinos of Mexican heritage, ranging from 50 to 91 years of age. The research survey was organized around two principal objectives: the first to assess the perception of old age by the respondent; the second to ascertain respondent perceptions of three types of institutionalized support, (1) the family, (2) the church, and (3) the government, in defining old age began at or just below the age of 60, in terms of institutional support. Sixty-two percent of the study respondents indicated that the family did not have an obligation to provide for them; 34 percent responded that the government should provide programs that would do "everything," "anything," or "just help" alleviate problems of their own or other minority aged. The authors report that the respondents had a limited knowledge of programs designed to aid the elderly.

Torres-Gil, Fernando.   *Los ancianos de la raza: A beginning framework for research, analysis and policy.* Unpublished masters thesis, Brandeis University, 1972.

An extensive review of the available literature on the Latino aged covering a six-year period which found fewer than 30 published and unpublished articles. Most of the articles dealt with housing and with communication or transportation as related issues. The author points out that all published articles were written by non-Chicanos and most studies were confined to Texas.

——————   *Political behavior: A study of political attitudes and political participation among older Mexican Americans.* Unpublished doctoral dissertation, Brandeis University, 1976.

The author undertook a study of 106 older Latinos of Mexican heritage in San Jose, California, ranging in age from 52 to 88 years. A principal finding of the study is that Latino elders of Mexican heritage cited lack of communication and fear or apprehension rather than ideological or intergenerational conflict as the major reason for not engaging in political activities, particularly those centering around identifiable "Chicano" concerns.

U.S. Congress, Senate Special Committee on Aging.   *Availability and usefulness of federal programs and services to elderly Mexican Americans.* Parts 1-5. Washington, D.C.: U.S. Government Printing Office, 1969.

These five hearings were held throughout the United States by the U.S. Congress, Senate Special Committee on Aging. The recurrent needs stressed throughout the hearings include language problems, lack of awareness of service programs, transportation, health care needs and housing. The reports stress that the reasons for under-utilization of services are often due to lack of outreach service by agencies, alienation resulting from impersonal bureaucratic procedures and the lack of the presence of bilingual/ bicultural personnel with service delivery systems. The reports provide a basic review of policy issues related to the Latino elderly.

Vélez, Carlos.   The aged and the political process. In Ascención Hernández and John Mendoza (Eds.) *Institute on aging: An orientation for Mexican American community workers in the field of aging.* Topeka, Kansas: National Chicano Social Planning Council, 1973.

The writer stresses that a contradiction exists for the Latino elders' inner social and cultural world and the cultural and social structures he or she encounters in the broader society.

Appendix B: The Research Instrument

Introduction to the Use of the Interview Guide*

This interview schedule is a *guide only*. As we discussed in training, there are sixteen major information categories, each with its own set of key information items. For example, "Category 1, Language and Background" has nine separate information items numbered 1 through 5c. Obviously you will ask some items, for example (2a), only if the respondent says he or she was born outside of the mainland USA. Obviously you will continue in the same way throughout the other major categories.

Because this is a *guide only*, each information item has been trimmed down to its barest form. As we discussed in training, you *are not to ask for the information in that way*. For example, information Item 1, in Category 1 in the English version says briefly, "1. Where were you born?" Item 5 says, "5. Which languages do you speak?" You will find the versions in your respective ethnic group languages, Spanish, Chamorro, Chinese, etc., are written in the same bare bones style. We expect you will add the necessary ethnically and locally appropriate language when you ask for the information.

Examples will help highlight what we mean. When you ask Item 1 in Category 1, we would expect you to say, "1. Could you please tell me the year you were born?" or "1. As a first question could I ask you to please tell me when you were born?" This latter way of asking Item 1 is probably better for those of you whose elders use other than the western calendar.

As we discussed in training, we do need as specific information as possible. We expect you to phrase the question properly, showing the correct manner of address as expected by the elders of your ethnic group. We want you to dig out the facts, but we want you to be gentle and respectful in the way you do this.

It would be important if maybe you took the long version of the interview guide—the 32-page version with all the complete instructions—along to your first two interviews. As you can see, all instructions and suggested ways to phrase the questions have been removed from the 11-page interview guide which follows. The reason for this is that the shorter guide is built to make it easier for you to record the information you get.

We will be debriefing you right after your first two interviews. We can work out any questions you might have at that time. From our discussion to this point, we are certain that you understand the basis of this guide. Now all that remains is to try it out for the first time.

* NOTE: These were the instructions issued verbally during the March 1975, interviewer training prior to the interviewer's first two interviews. The in-depth 32-page interview guide is on file at The Center on Aging, AoA Project Archives.

Interview Guide for AoA

Cross-Cultural Study of Minority Aged of San Diego (1974-1976)

**Center on Aging
School of Social Work
San Diego State University**

A. Interviewer # (   )
B. Interview # (   )

Minority Aged Interview Guide

Category 1.   Language and Background

1.   What year were you born?
2.   Where were you born?
2a.   When did you come to (mainland) USA?
3.   How many years have you lived in San Diego?
4.   How long have you lived in this (neighborhood/barrio/area/reservation)?
5.   What languages do you speak?
5a.   Which language do you usually speak?
5b.   Can you get by speaking English, if you have to? (yes, with difficulty, no)
5c.   Can you get by reading and filling out forms written in English? (yes, with difficulty, no)

Category 2. Family

6.   Are you married or have you ever been married?
7.   Do you have any family?
7a.   Where do your family members live?

	brother sister	children	grandchildren great- grandchildren	parents	other
same residence					
immediate neighborhood					
S.D. county					
outside S.D. county					
N/A					

8.   Do you see or have contact with relatives? (other than those living with you) If so, about how often? (per week or month, etc.)
9.   Would you like to see your relatives more often, about the same, or less often than you do now?
9a.   What are the things that keep you from getting together more often? Anything else?
9b.   Why would you prefer to see them less often?

Category 3. Education

10.   When you were young, did you have time to go to school?
10a. Could you tell me how many years of schooling you had?

Category 4. Employment

11.   What type of work did you (and/or your spouse) do most of your life?
12.   Are you (your spouse) employed presently?
12a. (IF EMPLOYED) Are you (your spouse) employed full time or part time?
12b. What kind of work do you (your spouse) do? (specify exact kind)
13.   (IF NOT EMPLOYED) Have you (your spouse) been employed in the past?
13a. About how long has it been since you (your spouse) have been employed?
13b. Would you (your spouse) like to work now?
13c. Full time or part time?
13d. What kind of work would you (your spouse) like to do? (specify)
13e. What difficulties have you (your spouse) had in finding employment? (specify)

Category 5.   General Problem Areas

14.   What would you say are the things that presently cause you the greatest difficulty? (list in order of priority)

Category 6.   Housing

15.   Do you own this house/apartment, rent it, help share the rent with another or does someone else take care of the rent/house payments?
16.   How long have you been living in this particular building/house/apartment/room?
17.   About how much do you pay per month for rent or mortgage payments?
18.   (IF RENTING) When you need repairs, can you get the landlord to do them without difficulty, with some difficulty, or is it almost impossible to get anything done?
18a.   What is it that you have difficulty getting done—what is the problem? (Probe—is there any other problem?)
19.   If you had the opportunity would you move out if you could?
19a.   Why do you feel that way? (Any other reasons?)

Category 7.   Neighborhood

20.   What do you think of this neighborhood as a place to live—would you say it is a good, fair, or poor place to live?
20a.   What are the things you like or dislike about this neighborhood?
21.   What are some of the important things, in your opinion, that make a good neighborhood? (Probe)

Category 8.   Health

22.   In general, would you describe your health as good, fair, or poor?
23.   Are there any particular problems or disabilities that bother you at the present time? (Probe—are there any other health problems, etc.?)
23a.   Have you received medical attention for this (these) problem(s)?
24.   Have you been a patient in a hospital, nursing home or other medical facility since becoming an older person?
24a.   Did you receive the care you needed?
24b.   Why didn't you receive the care you needed? (Probe)
25.   What do you feel are the major reasons older people sometimes do not go to a doctor or clinic even though something is bothering them? (Probe—any other reasons?)
26.   Do you know about MediCal and Medicare?
26a.   Have you ever used or are you now using either MediCal or Medicare?

Category 9.   Nutrition

27.   How many meals do you usually have every day?

28.   Can you describe the meals (food) you have on a typical day?

29.   Do you usually have your meals alone or with other people? If with others, with how many?

30.   Do you usually prepare meals for yourself or does some other person prepare them for you? (Who is that?)

31.   Do you require a special diet for your health?

32.   What do you think would most improve your meal times? Anything else?

Category 10.   Transportation

33.   What is your primary means of transportation?

33a.   Do you have your own car, borrow a car from someone or does another person usually drive you where you need to go?

34.   When you really need it, is some form of transportation usually available or not?

Category 11.   Finances

35.   How would you describe the financial position you (you and your spouse/your household) find yourself in—good, fair or poor?

36.   About how much is your average monthly income?

37.   Could you also tell me from which sources you (you and your wife/husband) presently receive income? (Probe—anything else?) (Ask about Social Security)

38.   Many older people do not have enough income to live on. What do you think could be done to change this situation? (Probe)

Category 12.   Who Helps?

39.   When you have difficulties, who is generally the person (or people) you usually go to first? (in order of preference)

39a.   Why do you turn to this person (these people)?

40.   I will mention some specific things that could possibly happen to you so that you might have to turn to someone for help. Could you tell me in each case to whom you would probably turn first?

	1*	2	3	4	5	6	7	8	9
If:									
(a) sickness hits you									
(b) it is important that you get somewhere quickly and you don't have the transportation									
(c) you are running short and need a few dollars									
(d) you need more than a few dollars									
(e) you are feeling lonely or something is bothering you and you need to talk to someone									
(f) you need help to do some work around the house that you are not able to do alone									
(g) you are short on food									

*1. yourself/no one; 2. family member; 3. friend; 4. neighbor; 5. agency/professional person; 6. member(s) of organized group; 7. other (specify); 8. D/K; 9. N/A

41. Is the person/or people you get most of your help from inside this neighborhood/barrio or from outside?

42. Are you ever called on to help or assist others?

42a. Would you say that you are asked to help others often, sometimes or very little?

42b. Who is it (which person or persons) that asks for your help?

42c. What kind of help do you give?

Category 13. Formal Assistance

43. Do you know of any agencies, organizations, clubs, etc., which help take care of (health needs, etc.) if the need arises?

43a. 1. Do you use or have you used any of these services or agencies, etc.?
(IF NOT)
2. Would you use this agency, service club, etc. if the need arose?

43b. 1. What did you like and/or not like about the service and way you were treated?
OR
2. Why would you not use this service, agency, etc.?

NEEDS	43) Knowledge name/describe agencies	43a) Use using or have used	would use	would not use	43b) Comments (extremely impt!!) positive (specify)	negative (specify)
1. health						
2. financial						
3. nutritional						
4. transportation						
5. counseling/ advising						
6. legal help						

44. Also, can you think of any kind of help which to your knowledge is not available but which you think is needed, either by yourself or by other people?

45. Can you think of any specific things that agency workers or other people providing services should know, or be aware of, that would help provide better services to (ethnic identifier) people?

46. Who do you think should be responsible for helping set up new services and/or making any changes of problems you may have suggested?

Category 14. Activities

47. What do you enjoy doing with your time? (Probe—anything else?)

48. These activities that you do—do you usually do them by yourself or with others, for example with family, friends, or as part of an organized group?

49. Are you a member of any organized groups or associations?

49a. Could you tell me the names of these groups or clubs and their purpose or function? (religious, political, ethnic, recreation, etc.)

49b. Are most of the members of these groups (list groups named) also (ethnic identifier) like yourself or are other people part of the group? (Note whether of same or mixed ethnicity.)

50. Are there special events, days, celebrations of feasts which are held to celebrate (ethnic identifier) holidays which you know about?

50a. What are they?

50b. How do you celebrate these?

51. Are you a member of a church or religious group?

51a. What church or religion?

52. Would you say that most of your friends and acquaintances are (ethnic identifier)?

Category 15. Cultural Values

53. What do you think determines when a person is considered old?

54. When you were a young person, do you remember what values and traditions you were taught about how an older person was to be treated?

55. How do you feel about the way you are now being treated as an older person? Is it different than you had expected—if so, in what ways?

56. Also, when you were a young person, do you remember the values and ways you learned about how (ethnic identifier) help each other during times of need?

57. How do (ethnic identifier) take care of each other today in times of need? Have you seen any changes taking place since you were young?

58. In regard to what we have discussed about (ethnic identifier) traditions and values concerning the help you give each other and what it means to be old, what would you recommend to (ethnic identifier) younger than yourself?

59. Do you think things in general, are getting better, the same, or worse for (ethnic identifier)?

59a. Why do you feel this way?

/ R. Valle & L. Mendoza |

Category 16.   Descriptive Information

(To be completed prior to start of interview or afterward, as appropriate.)

C.   Location of respondent's residence:

Ca.   SRA Code #

Cb.   MSA Code #

Cc.   Name of city, or community (if in city of San Diego)

Cd.   Nearest cross-street

D.   Ethnic designation of respondent

E.   Sex of respondent

F.   Number of contacts made in person and/or by telephone or letter:

Fa.   Contacts made in person (to include present interview)

Fb.   Contacts by telephone

Fc.   Contacts by letter

G.   Language of interview

H.   Specific "ethnic identifier" used during interview.

I.   Interviewer briefly describe physical setting

J.   Others present during course of interview

J1.   Did others help respondent or take part in the interview, and to what degree? (not at all, very little, some, great deal)

K.   Did respondent understand most questions quite well or was there much difficulty in understanding? (understood, some difficulty, great difficulty)

L.   Were there any particular questions or areas of the questionnaire to which the respondent was particularly sensitive? (explain)

M.   What was the social distance during course of the interview? For example: (1) Friendly/close throughout; (2) Began friendly/close—became less so; (3) Began formal/distant—became more friendly; (4) Formal/distant throughout; (5) Was rather hostile or unresponsive; (6) Other (specify).

N.   Do you have any other comments concerning this interview which may be useful to the study?

DEBRIEFING SCHEDULE

Introduction to the Use of the Debriefing Schedule

This debriefing guide is designed to be used by each of you with the interviewers of your respective ethnic groups. You will note that a number of the items are similar to some information items contained in Category 16, "Descriptive Information," in the interview guide. The intent is not to be repetitive, but rather to facilitate your in-depth probing around methodological and ethnic content items. We want to identify as many discrete bits of information as possible about the research process in action. We want to do the same about ethnic content. We want to bring to the surface what may be culturally taken for granted between the interviewer and respondent. We want to highlight the interviewer's natural skills as much as possible.

AoA Cross-Cultural Study on the Minority Aged

Debriefing Schedule (Finalized)

Interview Methodology Items

1. Overall time: TOTAL:

    actual interview   precontact   travel time   recording

2. Precontacts:
    How many (in person, by letter)?
    Who was used as door opener (were others used) e.g., by name?
    What kind of information was conveyed at the precontact?
3. Actual Interview:
    How did actual interview begin? (style, language used, starting point)
    How was nature of study, relationship of SDSU, AoA, goals of study handled?
    Areas of social difficulty/sensitivity?
    How was the use of the interview guide introduced?
4. Did interviewer give any information from own personal life? (yes, no)
4a. If yes, explore the kind of information shared.
5. Did interviewer give services (e.g., information and referral)? (yes, no)
5a. If yes, explore type of service given.
6. Was food/drink offered? (yes, no)
6a. Were any other types of exchanges made? (yes, no)